THE VIGILANT FUNDRAISER

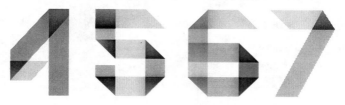

12 STEPS TO FUNDRAISING SUCCESS

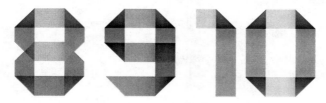

EDITED BY GEORGE STANOIS

"This book has captured what every fundraiser and volunteer needs to pay attention to for optimum results. I would encourage all fundraisers to include *The Vigilant Fundraiser* in their library but also to **make sure that staff at all levels read it**. Each of the 12 Steps could be a focus of discussion at your Board meetings or planning retreats."

GORD DURNAN, CFRE, FAHP
Board of Governors, *Nipissing University*
Chair, *Muskoka Community Foundation*

"**This book is a must read** both for newcomers to the field and veteran fundraisers, looking to keep their skills, methods and philosophies current and effective."

TOM SHAND
Executive Director,
Canadian Mental Health Association,
Alberta Division

"George Stanois has edited a great new book, *The Vigilant Fundraiser: 12 Steps to Fundraising Success.* **It's a tour de force.** As a direct response fundraiser, I was particularly taken with Chapter 7 by Liz Rejman. Pick up the book, read this chapter and make sure you're doing the right thing. It all starts with the right list."

STEVE THOMAS, CFRE
Chairman & Executive Creative Director
Stephen Thomas Ltd

Library and Archives Canada Cataloguing in Publication

Stanois, George, 1960-, author
      The vigilant fundraiser : 12 steps to fundraising success / George Stanois.

Includes index.
ISBN 978-1-927375-12-9 (pbk.)

      1. Fund raising. I. Title.

HG177.S73 2013   658.15'224   C2013-906383-8

The Vigilant Fundraiser:™ 12 Steps to Fundraising Success

Published by Civil Sector Press
Box 86, Station C, Toronto, Ontario, Canada M6J 3M7
Telephone: 416 345-9403
www.charityinfo.ca

Publisher: Jim Hilborn
Substantive Editor: Lisa MacDonald
Cover art and complete book design: John VanDuzer, wishart.net

THE VIGILANT FUNDRAISER:
12 STEPS TO FUNDRAISING SUCCESS

This book is dedicated to the thousands of professional fundraisers and tireless volunteers who I have had the privilege of working with over the course of my career.

It is also dedicated to **Kevin Allen** for giving me a chance.

The Vigilant Fundraiser got its start as the 12-Step Fundraising Program. Over the years I have developed a number of best practices I consider integral to the success of a fundraising program. I want to thank **Jim Hilborn** for encouraging me to take the program and create this book.

I am also indebted to all the authors who so generously shared their knowledge and **Lisa MacDonald** for her skills in pulling this labour of love together. I must also mention my good friend, **Bob Hanneman**, for his invaluable advice over the years.

My wife Dianne, and daughters, Chloe and Nastasia, deserve a very special thank you for allowing me to indulge my passion.

It's not work if you love what you do.

George Stanois
Toronto, ON
2013

TABLE OF CONTENTS

FOREWORD

I first met George Stanois in 1984, when he was transferred from the Canadian office of the firm we worked for to assist on a national church campaign in the U.S. George quickly fit in with this loud group of American consultants. Over the course of the campaign, George and I shared laughs, frustrations and more than a few pitchers of beer. At the end of that campaign, he returned to Toronto and I was sent to Britain for the Rotary International campaign.

In 1988 our paths crossed again, this time in Toronto. We had signed up to work for Kevin Allen at Navion Inc. We found Kevin to be a brilliant fundraiser and a confident, capable mentor, instructing us on designing capital campaigns, directing staff and managing a business. George excelled in the profession, successfully "working in the trenches" of capital campaigns, and developing a network of business friends and fundraising colleagues that stretched across Canada and the U.S. Throughout this period, we continued to share experiences, laughs, disappointments — and more than a few bottles of wine.

In 1996 I moved back to the U.S. and George became a partner at The Goldie Company, Canada's long-established and highly-esteemed fundraising consulting firm. Success followed George and in 2005 he assumed full ownership of the company. Since then, George's dynamic leadership style has defined The Goldie Company and the many services it now offers the nonprofit sector.

One of George's great gifts is his ability to cut through the "noise and fog" to clearly identify the real problems confronting an organization and then recommend realistic and reachable solutions. George has developed a 12-Step Fundraising program, a practical approach to fundraising designed to help nonprofits achieve success. I can vouch for its effectiveness, as I have used George's 12 steps in numerous presentations and instruction sessions and I can say that the steps are always well-received by development staff, Executive Directors and Board members.

These 12 steps form the basis of this book, The Vigilant Fundraiser. In The Vigilant Fundraiser, George and his guest authors cut through the noise and the fog so that a clear path to success is made possible for any nonprofit.

Chuck Birdie
Ashburn, VA
2013

Chuck Birdie is President of Lead2Succeed and has been working with nonprofit organizations for more than 30 years.

"CASE-LEADERSHIP-PROSPECTS-PLAN"

This is where it all started for me. It was one of the first things I learned as a fundraiser, and to this day I think it's both powerful and yet simple. You want to be a successful fundraiser? This is where you start: with a case for support; with leadership; your donor prospects and an executable plan to make it all happen.

When doing any kind of presentation, I still tend to structure the talk around these four headings. For me, it succinctly tells the story of how we get "from here... to there."

You also could consider this the core of the 12-Step Fundraising program. Somewhere along the way I realized that while Case-Leadership-Prospects-Plan were the anchors or starting point for the work I was doing, there was more to the fundamentals of fundraising that needed to be documented.

Fundraising is an organic process. You don't reinvent the wheel around the core activities of fundraising. You will find more success once you understand that there is a fundraising wheel and the 12-Step Fundraising program is what the wheel looks like. What is needed in managing this process is vigilance.

A vigilant fundraiser will look for opportunities _within_ the 12 steps that allow you to set your organization apart from all the others who do what you do. There is logic to what we do. I want to help fundraisers be more logical in their approach to revenue development. Being vigilant means using _all the steps_; executing 7 steps out of 12 isn't going to cut it. Recognize cause and effect. If your donations are declining, it means you aren't being vigilant.

Competition for both the dollar and the volunteer is high. Now, more than ever, is the time for being strategic _and_ more logical to save time and money. When I first came onto the fundraising scene in the early 80's there was very little competition. Now _every_ fundraising initiative needs to have a communication or awareness building component to it. That starts with a Case for Support – Step 1.

And talking about volunteers...well, it's all about the volunteers as far as I'm concerned. We need volunteers! Our volunteers act as door openers when an organization can't afford major gifts officers, they are our board members and our ambassadors in the community. They provide history and continuity when staff moves on and they are often the life blood that fuels an organization to grow and achieve.

I don't claim to have all of the answers, but the successes I've achieved have been accomplished through trial and error and applying a common sense approach to what I do. I have been using and sharing a philosophy — articulated in the 12-Step Fundraising program — for many years. In publishing this book, I wanted to give back what I've learned and encourage a best-practice approach with as many organizations as possible.

I approached this project as I do much of my work — by recruiting a team of skilled professionals who bring experience and passion to the challenge at hand. Thank you to Victoria White, John Phin, Jennifer Hilborn, Sarah Varley, Gina Eisler, Lee Pigeau, Liz Rejman, Paul Nazareth, Peter Barrow, Ed Sluga, John VanDuzer and Jim Watson for contributing their talent and time to this book.

These veteran nonprofit gurus understand that success depends on doing more with less. I think you'll find that in most professions, those who find success do so by keeping their eyes open and an ear to the ground. In my experience, the same can be said for the vigilant fundraiser.

George Stanois
2013

123
4567
8910
11 12

STEP

1

CASE FOR SUPPORT

"The most important document your organization will ever write."

A word from George...

I've heard it so many times:

"We have one... in _five_ different documents."

There is a reason that writing a Case for Support is Step 1 in the 12-Step Fundraising program. A Case for Support is quite simply the most important document your organization will ever write. It is the key document you will need to have in place when you set out to raise funds during an annual campaign; to fund a capital campaign or to state endowment needs and make requests for significant gifts. In addition, it will be your resource document when it comes time to write proposals and grant applications.

A Case for Support is essentially the rationale for supporting you based on both the factual background and history of your organization and on those beneficial, worthwhile services or solutions you provide to the community you serve every day.

When do you need a Case for Support? All the time — if you are a not-for-profit organization! Consider it a _business plan_ for donors. You want to show those _investors_ your organization is a worthy _investment_.

It must be the expression of your organization's credibility and integrity, and it must answer any question anyone could possibly raise about your organization:

- *Why is your organization different from similar service providers?*
- *What are the specific needs of the people / communities you serve?*
- *What impact are you making? Are you being successful?*
- *What are your priorities at this time? Your urgent needs?*
- *How will the funds raised be used?*
- *How will the funds specifically benefit those you serve? And the community?*

A well-written case will encourage people to ask you even <u>more</u> questions, as they will be eager to learn more about your organization and the wonderful things it does.
Of course, the main question you always want them to ask is, "How can I help?" Isn't that, after all, the goal of the Case for Support? In the end, a Case for Support is a call to action.

In my experience, what separates a great case from an ordinary Case for Support is that it doesn't simply express your funding goal — it weaves it into a compelling narrative that leaves no doubt as to the value of your organization and the immediate need for the prospective donor to get involved.

On a final note, let me address a couple of misconceptions about cases and about case writing.

First of all, remember that a Case for Support is a living document. Don't put it away under lock and key. It _will_ be your resource document for future reference. You can add and remove pages/material as necessary. And it will change with time. It is not static. You will have to revisit your original case from time to time as your organization evolves, achieves goals and reaches milestones. You will want to add these new achievements and you will want to revise it. You might even need to rewrite it. But never underestimate the importance of having a case document at the ready.

Also, it has been said that only the organization and its staff can write a good Case for Support. Not true. A professional writer will not only see your organization through fresh eyes, but also he or she will bring special training and language skills to the table, to articulate your case using the right words and the right tone that will positively reflect your organization while communicating your goals effectively.

Victoria White is a professional writer who has written countless cases and fundraising letters for a variety of nonprofit organizations. She understands the power of a well-written case. In Step 1 for the vigilant fundraiser, I've asked her to share some of her learned wisdom and skilled approach to case writing with you.

WRITING A POWERFUL CASE FOR SUPPORT

BY VICTORIA WHITE

Every not-for-profit needs a Case for Support. It is the cornerstone of all fundraising campaigns and provides a portfolio of your organization's amazing accomplishments. A Case for Support will describe your organization, inventory its achievements, demonstrate the need for funds, promote the cause and raise the organization's profile overall.

In addition, it can serve as an internal resource for your organization's communications, marketing, training and planning documentation. Because it is a summary of all that you are and all the wonderful things that you do, a Case for Support can be given to staff and volunteers alike so that they may properly communicate the organization's mission, vision and values when interacting with others. Think of it as a reference text, or the "company bible."

Researching and writing a Case for Support is always time well-spent, because a case can be repurposed and repackaged to suit other needs, such as case statements and "micro cases" tailored to specific campaigns. It can morph into a case summary for a grant proposal or lend content to major gift letters and other fundraising communications. When writing the case, however, never lose sight of its true purpose – to garner support for your organization, both moral and monetary.

CONSTRUCT A PERSUASIVE ARGUMENT

In order to realize that purpose, you must weave a compelling narrative, much as a fiction writer tells a tale. The Case for Support tells your organization's unique story to potential donors. It must draw your readers in and never let them doubt for a minute that your organization is the greatest and your cause the most worthy, which does not mean that you need to exaggerate or embellish. Just write with commitment and passion – the same commitment and passion that you bring to your work every day.

Whether your organization is saving lives, saving species or saving heritage, your appeal for support should inform every word you write and your persuasive argument must begin with the opening paragraph. Think of a Case for Support as a series of building blocks – each word, each paragraph and each section deliberately and steadfastly cultivating respect, admiration, credibility and trust, and ultimately creating a composite picture of your organization.

Or, if you prefer a musical analogy, consider the dynamic,

uplifting effect of a crescendo. When case writing, you are building an argument to substantiate a statement of need and to make a *justifiable ask*, which is the high note of your case. Your concluding statements form the coda.

Always be cognizant of your intent as you write. Connect your opening words to your need and your ask. If you maintain this clarity of purpose as you write, you will be able to choose what you should include in your case and what you could easily omit. By the time your potential donor reaches your financial request, his or her support is all but assured.

BALANCE IS EVERYTHING

To achieve balance you must craft your document with care. That means laser-like attention to language, tone and style. Precision matters. Don't be vague, don't overstate with excessively emotional language and, above all, don't plead. Avoid insider jargon that your donors will not understand. While your potential donors are intelligent, well-informed people, they may not be aware of terminologies that are part of your everyday life.

Explain obscurities – make data and stats relevant and meaningful to the overall argument. Never take for granted that they will be understood by simply plopping them into a bulleted list with no elaboration. Chances are that the point you are trying to make will be lost. It is your job to connect the dots for the reader.

A well-argued case may be logical, rational and full of great supporting statistics, but it can fall flat if it doesn't stir the soul's capacity for compassion. People do not give to causes, to arguments, or to bricks and mortars. People give to people. Studies now suggest that we humans are actually hardwired to be kind, so tap into that part of the human psyche that prompts us to help one another.

One of the most effective ways to do this is to use anecdotal material – include real-life stories about people or communities that your organization has helped. These may be quotes, testimonials or brief accounts embedded in the narrative. Just use these stories sparingly, avoiding sentimentality and emotionalism. An overly maudlin case is as ineffective as a dry and abstract one. You must appeal to both hearts and minds.

What you are trying to achieve, is that golden middle ground. A balanced case will state the need clearly while calling upon your readers' desire to help others and to give back to the community. A case has to appeal to two types of donors: those for whom statistics hold the most sway and those who are motivated by empathy. Anchor your case on facts, statistics and realities, but illustrate them with stories that highlight positive resolutions and outcomes resulting from your organization's efforts.

Here are a few more "best practices" to bear in mind

when writing a Case for Support, because these elements are often overlooked or given short shrift: don't ignore your organization's beginnings, however humble; don't forget about the people who make the organization work; and don't underestimate the importance of a powerful concluding statement.

HIGHLIGHT YOUR HISTORY

Never be afraid to give your donors a history lesson. There seems to be a growing trend among organizations to downplay their history in their documentation and on their websites. Brevity is a good thing in this fast-paced world, but if your potential donors don't know why your organization was founded – what event, what motivating factor ignited an individual or a group of individuals to act – then isn't a critical piece of information being lost? *Who were the founders? What was the catalyst – the original spark that drives your organization to this day?* You never know what will resonate with a potential donor and generate a dona-tion. As an example, can anyone think of the *Make-A-Wish Foundation* without recalling the story of *"The First Wish"* and little Christopher James Greicius?

Your history is what marketers call your "unique selling proposition," or the factor presented as the reason that one product or service is *different* from that of the competition. Normally, we do not talk about competition in the not-for-profit world, but consider this: your organization addresses a particular issue in the community, so you should be emphasizing that in your case. For example, if your mission is to support stroke survivors transitioning back to community life as opposed to stroke prevention and stroke research, the story of how your organization was founded could help to clarify that.

Of course, you won't be writing pages and pages of historical background. If you have a chronology or timeline, great! Use it as a guide or include it as an appendix. Keep it brief, but don't short change your organization either. Tell your story with pride. Just tell it succinctly.

IT'S A TEAM EFFORT

While the organization is the hero or heroine of the story, always remember to roll the credits for the cast of hardworking supporting characters – *your people*. Talk about your staff's dedication and those wonderful volunteers without whom you would not accomplish half the things you do. If the axiom is true (that people give to people), then it is equally true that the individuals who make up your team and make the organization work day after day will be of interest to potential donors.

Mention the number of volunteers and the number of volunteer hours. Include a quote or a testimonial from a volunteer or a staff member. Some of the most remarkable and touching stories will come from your team on the front line of service delivery. Stories of people helping others are inspiring, encouraging us to help, to give back, and to be the very best that we can be too.

Make sure your people are part of the story.

A POWERFUL CONCLUSION

You know that feeling of satisfaction when you come to the end of a good yarn? Unfortunately, some cases fall flat on the final page, as if the writer, exhausted, just wanted to hurriedly wrap it all up. The ask has been made, so why say more?

A good case will leave a potential donor knowing that he or she must *do* something. A great case will bring that potential donor back to the beginning. If you started your case with an individual's story, then refer to it again. If you led with a startling statistic, refer to it. Always bring your reader full circle.

Write the best possible final paragraph you can. If that means you end up having to rewrite your first paragraph, so be it. The order in which you write is irrelevant, as long as the case feels complete and delivers its powerful message when all is said and done. The final paragraph of your case is just as important as the opening paragraph. Make sure your words pack an unforgettable punch.

Writing a Case for Support for your organization is as

much about storytelling as it is about raising funds. Like all good stories, a Case for Support should grab the attention of readers right away, compel them to continue reading, and work its magic until the very last line. A great Case for Support will leave potential donors eagerly asking, *"Where do I sign up?"* Or better still, *"How much can I give?"*

A Case for Support states your funding goal, but it also reflects your organization through its style, structure, tone and language. When written in fresh, powerful language, it can banish donor fatigue and kindle (or rekindle) enthusiasm for your organization.

FUNDRAISING
STRATEGY

---

*"It's time to plan your work
and work your plan."*

A word from George...

To me, a vigilant fundraiser is someone who takes a strategic approach in the execution of their fundraising program. They understand that resource development is a <u>process</u> and as such is willing to take the time to apply rigour, measurement and structure to develop a fundraising strategy. I've always thought that Jim Watson said it best in his advice to "...plan your work and work your plan." But let's face it. Not everyone is good at planning. In that case, keep it simple.

There is an exercise I like to do that helps an organization to create a timeline for their fundraising efforts. We get a calendar, put it up on the wall and start listing activities and deliverables against real dates. Then we work backwards, creating a list of activities in a reasonable timeline, which will allow the fundraising team to successfully execute their fundraising plan. Is it rocket science? No. It's planning.

*Like **John Phin** points out in Step 2 — successful fundraising doesn't <u>just</u> happen.*

DEVELOP A FUNDRAISING STRATEGY

BY JOHN PHIN

Fundraising doesn't just happen. Your organization isn't so well-endowed with visibility and funding that it can afford not to pay attention to what it takes to operate a great fund development initiative. Every organization must have a collection of activities through which donors and other supporters can help the organization.

Your fundraising strategy or "the plan," addresses the dollars the organization requires over a period of time (arguably five years) from fundraising, sponsorship, and in-kind activity to deliver its programs and services. It outlines and organizes fundraising in terms of leadership, lines of authority, and types of fundraising that your organization can realistically do. It sets out the responsibilities of staff, governance and fundraising volunteers. It recommends action that is ambitious and sufficiently demanding to guard against complacency and inactivity.

The "ideal" plan will revolve around classic fundraising, organized by committees of volunteers and supported by staff. Major gift fundraising focuses on priority areas like special programs and services, capital building or renovation needs. Money from annual giving initiatives (special events, third party fundraising, gaming, and an internal campaign) will support ongoing costs. A planned giving initiative completes the fundraising program.

PURPOSE

Fund development is, by definition, the integration of fundraising, volunteerism, and communications activities that rally the organization's constituents around helping the organization achieve its mission in the community. Also, like any other department in your organization, fund development must strive for success. This requires determination to be noteworthy for your work by:

- *Identifying prospective donors and cultivating their interest and willingness to financially support the organization.*
- *Identifying and recruiting volunteers to provide their time and talents at a deeply personal level to benefit your organization's programs and services.*
- *Creating giving and volunteering opportunities that reflect your institutional priorities, with senior management and the board represented in every interaction.*
- *Managing creative solicitation and recruitment processes, ensuring philanthropic objectives are met and earned benefits are delivered.*

- *Conducting fundraising activities legally, ethically, and at well-recognized standards.*
- *Providing superior training in fundraising and volunteerism at every opportunity.*
- *Delivering on measureable commitments of time, talent, and dollars raised toward advancing your organization's objectives.*
- *Supporting your own organization with strong management of donor records, gift processing capacity, database manipulation, research activities, and strategic planning.*

OBJECTIVES

Resource development is a process. It integrates all of the approaches that result in the maximum gift of time, talent, and treasure from your various constituencies. The fund development program, as led by the vigilant fundraiser, achieves results by paying attention to some basic principles of fundraising and volunteerism, and by using effective fundraising, communications and engagement activities to their fullest potential.

The "plan," for its duration, will pay attention to these key activities, but never forget the overall objective — raise the money! Don't get so involved in the process that real fundraising gets lost. Build the program one year at a time.

Align people and their talents to give your program stability and the potential for growth. Organize traditionally under the broad categories of:

- *Annual Giving*
- *Major Gifts*
- *Planned Giving*

Give the program life by including a strong volunteer strategy under the banner of "community engagement." Fundraising can't exist in a vacuum, so make sure your communications program supports prospective donor identification, cultivation, solicitation, and steward-ship initiatives. Communication ought to align with your organization's strategic direction, so take advan-tage of this particular strength. All of this should be anchored with solid administration of your own fund development team.

Focus on aggressive donor acquisition, renewed stewardship of current support, inaugurating creative giving opportunities, meeting the immediate financial need and preparing for a secure financial future, and broadening the organization's scope of influence.

AGGRESSIVE DONOR ACQUISITION

Treat donor acquisition as a marketing exercise, and remember that donors are not forever. For your organi-zation to rely on a continuing number of well-qualified prospective donors, you'll need to establish acquisition programs to capture donors. Special events, third-party fundraising, internal (family) solicitation programs, community and volunteer engagement strategies ensure you have a continuing supply of potential donors.

RENEWED STEWARDSHIP

Focus on donor retention as a foundational strategy. Hopefully, you're fortunate to have a cohort of supporters and long-standing donors, with relationships well-rooted in your organization's mission and vision. These relationships were established painstakingly, and you can learn much from how these connections were made. Stewardship is the process whereby your organization seeks to be worthy of continued philanthropic, sponsorship, or volunteer support through recognition and appreciation activities, gift acknowledgement, sponsorship fulfillment, and volunteer engagement. This is how we bind donors to our cause. Highlight the outcomes of their support and celebrate philanthropy. In the process you will demonstrate to your constituents that they are making a difference.

INAUGURATING CREATIVE
GIVING OPPORTUNITIES

Find many ways for your donors to give. A planned giving initiative will open the possibility of gifts in the form of assets (property), and will encourage bequests. Third-party fundraising creates opportunities for community-based organizations, families, and other supporters to raise money on your behalf. Staff, board and the families that take part in your programs and services, are all potential donors who should be asked for their financial or other support.

MEETING IMMEDIATE NEEDS
AND PREPARING FOR THE FUTURE

Get your fund development plan authorized by the board, and be empowered to raise the money necessary for your organization to exist in the community. Create an Endowment, either managed by your organization of through the community foundation. It's an often-overlooked tool that you may have had for some time, and a giving opportunity for the right donor.

BROADENING YOUR SCOPE OF INFLUENCE

Participate in discussions with provincial leaders to strengthen funding of your programs and set the stage for infusions of capital dollars. Build a "Government Relations" program into your portfolio to maintain excellent relationships with ministers and officials. Your plan should include adopting cultivation initiatives to position your organization for future funding solicitation and to capture government's attention as its primary resource on issues dealing with your area of expertise.

Repurpose your volunteer resources to also function in "community engagement" and build an army of supporters. It's a tactical shift from a narrow view of volunteerism to a broader perspective and a process that can build relationships with community members who will work side by side with you as an ongoing partner in every way imaginable. Use this approach to enhance and increase your cultivation activities and raise the visibility of your organization as a charity of choice.

TACTICS

Every initiative and activity should be well-planned, strategic, and focused on advancing your organization's mission. A vigilant fundraiser moves quickly when an opportunity is presented. The interplay between deliberate and thoughtful work and seizing opportunities makes for a very dynamic program. As you go about your business, be committed to:

- *A donor-centered approach to philanthropic fundraising and volunteering*
- *A business benefit approach to sponsorship solicitation*
- *A program characterized by teamwork, collaboration, and a values-driven approach to problem solving*
- *Practices that are open to scrutiny and accepting of improvement*
- *Operating at the highest professional standards*

IN SUMMARY

Grow the annual giving program. Be involved in prospect identification and acquisition. Conduct and manage at least one signature special event, and be determined to do it well. Participate in allowable gaming activities. Seek the support of your organization's "clients." Develop a roster of prospect cultivation activities and ask for help from third-party activities.

Be bold and deliberate in major gifts. Conduct prospect identification exercises among your Board and senior volunteers. Put human resources and money toward an inquisitive research initiative. Write great proposals that capture the imagination and challenge donors to respond. Manage solicitations well and ensure your volunteers are confident that the information they have is the best and most accurate. Always have a list available of programs and capital needs that donors can fund, and renew that list annually.

Recognize that planned giving is a long-term investment and one that will help your organization. Strive to create awareness of charitable gift planning among all of your donor groups. Use planned giving as a platform for stewardship activities. Seriously investigate creating an endowment program.

Manage your fund development shop well. Invest time writing policies and procedures. Make sure your records are current, safe and confidential. Create a timetable of activity for your resource development program and stick to it. Inaugurate a dynamic stewardship and recognition program for which you will be renowned.

Engage the community. Be externally oriented. Seek to match what you do with the philanthropic interests of your donors, and then ask what they can do for you. Train your fundraising volunteers well and give the community permission to support your organization. Conduct tours if you run a facility. Recruit speakers who are experts from among your program staff to talk about what they do. Get the Board to tell stories about "their" organization.

Communicate. Broadcast your message. Make sure your key messages are known by everyone inside your organization, and let them tell everyone they know. Use every publicity and promotion tactic available. Use social media (just make sure you don't overestimate its effectiveness). Create a great Annual Report that tells your story and use it in proposals, speaking engagements, and special events.

Don't ignore government. Most Canadian charities have some stream of funding through a government program or initiative. Report well. Liaise with government's representatives, especially your provincial representative. Cultivate relationships with government departments that don't currently fund your organization.

Recruit a Resource Development Committee from the board and invite membership from people with a view to the wider community. When times are tough, it's great to have help moving fundraising initiatives forward. Recruit full and active (not honorary) "campaign" committees focused on fundraising, and give them the mandate to pursue their job with enthusiasm and purpose.

STEP

SPECIAL
EVENTS

---

*"A special event is the
Trojan horse of fundraising. It helps
to build awareness and get you involved
in other things."*

A word from George...

It happens all the time. When meeting someone new, I identify myself as a fundraiser and then the question comes — "What events are you involved in?"

Like it or not, the public's perception of fundraising is very much tied to events. In the nonprofit world, a special event is the Trojan horse of fundraising. It helps to build awareness and at the same time gets you involved in other things. This is one reason special events hold the position of Step 3 in the 12 Step Fundraising plan; the other reason is that the successful execution of a fundraising event is tied to many elements of being a vigilant fundraiser.

Special events require you to be strategic. First, they should be considered as part of an organization's overall fundraising strategy. Whether you decide to host a special event really depends on your particular organization: its mission, values, vision and culture. Given your organization's purpose and reason for being, is hosting special events imperative to raise funds? Or would an event be a novelty, something that your organization has yet to attempt but is now considering? Only you can decide what is appropriate for your organization.

Once you have decided that you want to include special events in your portfolio of fundraising strategies (either regular events, such as an annual gala, luncheon or run, or the occasional event that targets a specific objective), then the vigilant fundraiser must begin to plan and do research well in advance. Expect to do as much due diligence as you would with any other project your organization undertakes. Hosting a special event might seem like a lighthearted and enjoyable project (and it should definitely be appealing, pleasurable and rewarding for the invitees), but special event planning is not for the faint of heart and must be taken seriously, for it demands strong organizational skills and much patience.

Even after the event, the vigilant fundraiser knows that the work is not yet done. Time and care must be taken to evaluate the event's success. Budget figures will help you to measure quantifiable success, but post-event discussions with the various committees and those involved will complete the picture. Post-event evaluation and analysis is critical: it will help you and your organization to make sound decisions with regard to the hosting of future events.

Experienced event planners **Jennifer Hilborn** and **Sarah Varley**, might argue that the event audit is the single most important tool in the vigilant fundraiser's arsenal to ensure that any organizational event is meeting its objectives. In Step 3, they share best-practice tips and tactics for creating an event that does more than earn money for your organization's coffers. Your event can also make a positive impact on the community around you.

THE VIGILANT FUNDRAISER

SPECIAL EVENT BEST PRACTICES

BY JENNIFER HILBORN AND SARAH VARLEY

Who doesn't love a party? To many of us, an event can represent the most exhilarating and challenging aspect of the fundraising year. But events are more than just a fun diversion from the day-to-day of our usual jobs. Events are expensive and work-intensive. They can sap the energy of staff, donors, and even key stakeholders. That said, when done right, nothing reaches and connects with people more effectively and powerfully than an event.

WHY EVENTS?

Events arguably will help *build the profile* of your organization and this enhanced profile may expose the cause to new and bigger audiences – ultimately advocating for your cause and raising more money.

Events also help you to *position your organization* as different from the competition. For example, there are many cancer charities and causes. What makes any given one different? Your event should bring that difference to life in a clear and positive way.

As powerful experiences, events will often *mobilize attendees to act* on behalf of your cause. Attendees may be driven to speak about your social issue to their networks, or even start volunteering for your organization. The individual that starts off working at the coat check at a gala could evolve into a long-term, weekly volunteer for your nonprofit, based solely on their experience at your event.

Events help *build a donor base and a list* from which to market to year-round. The individual who is invited to sit at a table at a gala dinner, or join a foursome, might know nothing about your organization when they agreed to attend, but the excitement of the event will help you to forge a more meaningful connection with them. Their participation is an opportunity for you to ask permission to talk to them again throughout the year.

Events allow you to *reach out to the community*, getting support and buy-in for initiatives you champion, bringing on new community partners, not only for your events, but potentially for your organization as a whole.

Finally, events can help *raise funds* – often undesignated – that can be directed where they are needed most.

RUNNING AN EFFECTIVE EVENT

Some events can be resource-zapping, work-intensive efforts, for which the return on investment for the organization is debatable. Thinking of the impact of events in your fundraising efforts, do any of the following scenarios sound familiar?

1. *You have been running an event for several years and question if it still delivers on your stated objectives.*

2. *You are part of an organization that does not currently have a signature event but senior management thinks you should have one.*

3. *Key stakeholders and staff are growing weary of your existing event.*

4. *The fundraising for, or attendance to, your event has hit a plateau or has even started to decline.*

5. *Your organization has inherited a third-party event that you fear you cannot handle.*

6. *Your organization has gone through a change in direction or leadership, making you question if your event still works.*

7. *Your audience is changing and your event hasn't changed with it.*

8. *The landscape around your event has changed such that your event has been compromised.*

9. *You have lost a key asset — i.e. a celebrity spokesperson — that used to make your event successful.*

10. *Despite pressure to host an event, you have a sense that this is not the most effective way to achieve your organization's objectives.*

If any of these statements ring true for you, then your organization might stand to benefit from some best practices in event management; primarily, an *event audit*.

Even if an event is currently performing the way it should, event success can be cyclical and audiences are always changing. The vigilant fundraiser will stay ahead of the curve and anticipate change by regularly conducting an event audit. While audits and planning lack the glamour and excitement of events themselves, they pave the way for events that meet their stated objectives — pleasing executive directors, board members and donors alike.

An event audit looks at both internal and external factors that affect the health and strength of your event. It helps to determine how your event can evolve as your organization changes, if an event should be reinvented, or if the idea of an event should be entirely put to rest. In short, the process of the event audit uses best practices in events to reveal your organization's recommended next steps in relation to planning and managing a fundraising event; and most importantly leaves you and your event accountable to your organization's mission and objectives.

CONDUCTING AN EVENT AUDIT

1. Set realistic, measurable, and prioritized objectives: Make it achievable. Outrageous objectives lead to failure. Acknowledge limitations, start small and build; better to under-promise and over-deliver. Prioritized objectives help in moments of indecision, or when there are differing opinions; by revisiting priorities, one can be more decisive. Furthermore, by setting outrageous objectives, we usually have to invest more, and therefore risk more. By being clear and realistic about the objectives and the time and investment required to achieve them, you will minimize the inherent risk that events present.

2. Organizational control and buy-in: Owning your event and having buy-in from key stakeholders at your organization is an essential key to success. Ownership is control. Furthermore, buy-in from all key stakeholders helps manage expectations and secure support for decisions along the way — so make sure to include key stakeholders in planning meetings from the start.

3. Manage the time commitment for volunteers and staff: Events are resource-draining; you don't want key staff and volunteers spending all their time struggling to make an event a success. Time is money; depending on your objectives, those individuals could better spend their time doing other things for the organization.

4. *Embrace realistic logistics:* As with objectives, take on an event that is easy for your organization to manage. Bigger and more complex is not always better. Understanding your organization's resource-based limitations can help you to determine the right kind of event to create. Small teams with limited resources or limited outside help should not feel the need to take on events that close down city streets, or involve huge outlays of cash in advance. Sometimes small and simple is the best choice.

5. *Set manageable and realistic timelines:* Give yourself time to pull off the event. Depending on the event scope, you will need different amounts of time; but not many significant events can be pulled off with less than three months planning time. If you plan on having sponsors at your event, you will require at least six months lead time prior to the event to secure them.

6. *Pick the right time for your event:* Don't pick a time when lots of competing priorities exist within your organization, or when the marketplace is cluttered with other events.

7. *Anticipate and plan for growth:* Unless this is a one-off event, for the amount of time you spend developing it, you need to create an event that is repeatable and can grow over time. You can build on it each year, learn from mistakes and attract new attendees and new sponsors.

8. Customize the event for your target audience: Does the event match what your target audience wants? Would they enjoy attending it? What else is happening for them at this time? How is your target audience changing? Is your event changing with them? Are there new audiences you want to reach through this event? Everything from theme, timing and location, to music, messages, and menu will say that you had them in mind — or didn't.

9. Clearly define roles and responsibilities: An event plan that clearly defines roles and responsibilities protects the individuals and the team from assumptions that, "you were responsible for that" and the ever-present threat of burn out.

10. Measure success: Positive feedback, concrete analysis, and proof of success are all critical to repeating an event. This last point is so vital to your event's success that it warrants a deeper look.

THE IMPORTANCE OF METRICS

If a successful event is one with realistic objectives, then it is equally important that we clearly define the metrics that will prove that you achieved those objectives. Metrics allow you to be accountable, improve processes, and returns.

But defining your metrics won't matter, if you do not build in the mechanisms by which to measure them. You need to think about this when you develop your event, not after the fact. Objectives are worthless if you have no quantifiable or qualitative measures in place to prove you achieved them, or to help to determine where improvements could have been made or things could have been done better.

Media clippings and value, attendance numbers, web traffic, and funds raised are all measureable and reportable.

It's harder to measure qualitative objectives, but they may be the very stats that prove the deeper efficacy of your event efforts. For instance, how do you determine if people see your issue as more important than before the event, or if people were moved and inspired by your event? If you are hoping for a change in audience behaviour, then you need a call-to-action and a mechanism to measure when that action is happening. The most common way to deal with many of these issues is to put a survey in place asking people to comment on these things. The web is a great tool for this.

Also, how do you know if sponsors feel appreciated and valued for their contribution? An obvious indicator of sponsor approval is renewal, but if you want to know whether the event worked for them before their contract is expired, you need to consult them. You would be amazed at how many properties and events do not follow-up with their partners.

Your sponsors will thank you for it.

Some of the people that you might be pleased and proud to be accountable to include: the media, your Board, the attendees, prospective sponsors, existing sponsors, donors, and the community.

At the end of the day, when all the chairs are stacked, lights are out, and fundraising dollars are tallied, it is your relationships with stakeholders and donors that matter most. Good experiences foster good relationships and these good relationships are at the root of effective fundraising and making a powerful difference for your cause.

STEP

4

DONOR RECOGNITION
AND STEWARDSHIP

"The statement I hear most frequently is, 'The only time I hear from that organization is when they want more money!'"

A word from George...

When it comes to stewardship of donors there is no, "one size fits all" solution. It depends on the capacity of the organization, the types of fundraising being done and the level of engagement wanted by your donors. Yet, stewardship is a critical step in executing a successful fundraising program. The last thing a vigilant fundraiser wants to hear is that one of their donors has said, "The only time I hear from that organization is when they want more money!"

The donor-organization relationship does not end with a charitable gift – rather it begins at that point.

Responsible and effective stewarding of donors is what a nonprofit practices (or should be practicing) from the moment a gift is received until the relationship with the donor has ended. Excellent stewardship is about cultivating and supporting relationships with individuals, groups and organizations, and is expressed through the cooperative planning and management of charitable resources.

Understanding stewardship and how to build and sustain bonds with donors is integral to philanthropy. The relationships that you cultivate can be enhanced and sustained over time to the benefit of your mission and the well-being of all concerned – including your donors.

Being vigilant in your stewardship practice is recognizing

that to build a bond with your donor you must do more than send out a thank-you note. The thank-you is the primary response to receiving a gift; however, the main objective of stewardship is to secure the next gift. The organization must deliver what they promise and demonstrate that they truly appreciate the support of donors.

According to Julia Emlen's "Intentional Stewardship: Bringing Your Donors to Their Highest Level of Philanthropy," a good stewardship program seeks to promote eight key behaviours among donors:

1. Giving regularly
2. Giving to priorities
3. Giving in useable ways
4. Giving to capacity
5. Feeling recognized
6. Willingness to participate
7. Spreading the message
8. Bringing others along

Because donors are often your biggest public ambassadors — keep them engaged by making sure they know what's going on and have relevant information at their fingertips. Send them your newsletter, via email or print, as long as it is their preference. Send them holiday and/or birthday cards. Invite them to upcoming organization events. Send newspaper clippings on topics that will pique their interest. Be proactive and ask questions.

When it comes to stewardship, there are five things a vigilant fundraiser can do to distinguish your organization from other nonprofits:

1. Thank donors promptly and warmly.
2. Give donors information about how gifts are or will be used.
3. Honour the intentions of donors.
4. Use a donor's gift how you told the donor it would be used.
5. Recognize the donor in the way you agreed to.

In a 2010 Goldie survey of major donor cultivation and recognition practices of charities in Canada, "Dodging Tough Times: How Stewardship Programs Can Make All The Difference," results indicated that those organizations with a stewardship program in place were cushioned from the impact many nonprofits faced during challenging economic times. Think of it this way: in good economic times a donor typically gives to five different charities, in bad times that same donor will cut back on their donations, only giving to two organizations. What do you think impacts their decision on who to cut?

Gina Eisler understands the importance of stewardship. She has been a leading voice in helping charities to develop best practice in their stewardship methods. In Step 4 she shares her own journey of learning the lesson of the need for rigorous and organized recognition practices.

DONOR RECOGNITION AND STEWARDSHIP: LESSONS LEARNED THE HARD WAY

BY GINA EISLER, MA, CFRE

Imagine yourself taking two octogenarians on a tour of "their" hospital and its sadly outdated maternity unit (it's a cultivation tour). They request to see the room they affectionately dedicated to their long-deceased parents. This was long before Blackberries, so I did not have the time or ability to call the Intensive Care Unit (ICU) to let them know I would be bringing the donors that funded part of the Unit to see the result of their very generous gift – suddenly turning this into a stewardship visit.

Had I been able to initiate contact, I would have learned and spared them, and I, the incredible shock and disappointment of seeing that their significant donation to furnish a life-saving ICU suite had become a dark and dismal storage room for broken furniture and outdated intensive care equipment. I felt their loss of trust, disappointment, and saw the hurt on their faces; almost as if something dishonest had happened.

51

In fact — it had. In good faith, they made a significant pledge, and paid it in full, to the hospital and the Foundation. A plaque was installed bearing their name, and the names of their beloved deceased parents, for all to witness. Unfortunately, the nurses, physicians, maintenance department and even administration of ICU were probably not aware of the agreement made between these donors and the Foundation.

Despite happening fifteen years ago, the look on their faces haunts me to this day, and has inspired me to try to implement better stewardship plans, policies and then — to actually follow through on them. The questions arising from this sad encounter stay with me and are forefront every time I create a gift agreement. I hope I can help others avoid the loss of a donor's trust by sharing some simple and yet critical questions.

1. *Whose responsibility is it to inform the Foundation/charity and then the donor that a room has had its function change?*

2. *Did the gift agreement specify another space would host the recognition?*

3. *Was there a time limit on the dedication of the room/recognition? Long gone are "in perpetuity" donor recognition opportunities — especially when rooms/space is offered.*

4. *Is anyone assigned to do an annual "walk about" with a spreadsheet detailing*

donor gifts and recognition?

5. *Did the organization's board/committee responsible agree to a policy that space /buildings/areas could be used to recognize donors? If yes, is this in writing?*

6. *Who regularly evaluates the suggested gift amount allocated to each space? Hopefully, it is not the amount the last chair person gave as they "suggested" that their name be on the door of the board room. Each area must be evaluated based on its use and its "sexiness" within the organization (volume of visitors who will see the name). In sports marketing this is a given. It has taken philanthropy longer to be able to truly acknowledge the value we are giving to donors when we create signage that bears their name.*

7. *Last but not least, consult the Canada Revenue Agency when in doubt. Is it sponsorship or philanthropy?*

I wish I could say that this was the only time a hospital room had been changed from one that a donor proudly told their family and friends about, into one that became storage; but it isn't. Nor is it the only time that I cringed, back-pedaled apologetically and had to rebuild a relationship (and it takes so much longer to re-establish trust when large gifts are involved) after discovering that a promise to a donor had not been fulfilled.

Yet, charities blame donors for not making pledge payments, for changing their estate plans and for not referring them to their friends, family and colleagues. For some reason, we forget that philanthropy is about giving and not sales, it is voluntary and not mandatory, and it is these gifts that fulfill our missions. Without philanthropy, our organizations cease to exist, and those we serve remain in need.

Like most philanthropic / development functions, the line between art and science is blurry. Stewardship must come from the heart, encompassing creativity, imagination, and passion – the art. However, each donor's stewardship plan must be written (the science with art) based on the size of the gift, the reporting requirements (e.g. for banks, corporations and foundations), the mission related accomplishments due to the funds, the need for the future payments and what they will accomplish, and of course – the measurements and factors utilized to prove the outcomes resulting from the financial commitment of the donor.

A NEED FOR CHANGE

When speaking to people at conferences or during a consulting session, I have discovered that few Foundations or development departments have agreements in place that address stewardship needs. Eventually the space will be needed when the room / space / building needs to be replaced and a new donor thanked for *their* very generous gift. What system will ensure that the previous donor continues to be honoured? It begs the question – who is doing this while we are all out trying to raise money? What vigilant charities are excelling at stewardship and what are they doing?

It was because of several similarly bad experiences that a number of seasoned professional fundraisers in Ontario were led to spend a Saturday lamenting poor stewardship practices and trying to uncover how we could execute far better stewardship for donors. The day resulted in a national survey designed to capture what was currently being done (special events, impact reports, etc.), what best practices have been learned, and most importantly – when the economy is down, are people still committed to their causes?

It was noted (more than once) that fifteen years ago, none of us had ever seen a posting for a "Stewardship Officer;" as we continuously battle cost per dollar raised issues and an increasingly skeptical public. If we must hire people to write reports to document where each dollar has been spent and they must be done for each donor at a major gift level, how does the organization account for this? The person is critical for future gifts (and pledge payments to be fulfilled), but how do we explain this to direct response donors?

The Goldie Company worked with The Hilborn Group to conduct this national electronic survey and publish the results into a very useful report. Two hundred and seven charities participated in the survey with the majority of respondents from central and western

Canada. In 2009, despite market crashes and a lot of economic bad news, 56% of responding charities had an *increase* in donations and 81% had a stewardship program that had been in place for five years or more. The organizations with stewardship staff are raising more money ($1 million plus annually). This is not surprising. The more revenue you bring in, the more staff you can hire. Regardless, the survey illustrated the need for someone to report to donors that their gifts are being used wisely and are making a difference. The person doing the reports must be a donor-centred, creative employee with ability to both write and conduct research and the task should be included as part of their job description.

Events were not deemed to be the most important stewardship activity – reports and communicating face-to-face (for major donors) are by far the top way of communicating results to supporters. Top success factors included having a strong Case for Support, an up-to-date database, cultivation plans, media communications that report results, a fundraising committee and well-informed major donors. Each factor can make a huge difference in a donor fulfilling their pledge, making an additional gift – or even adding the organization to their estate plans.

TIPS ON STEWARDING DONORS

It should go without saying that regular contact (a few times a year; more if they wish it), follow-through on what has been promised, honesty at all costs, and mean-ingful information are the best methods of keeping a relationship with a donor alive and well. For example, sending the golf tournament wrap-up information to a senior citizen that doesn't golf is not appropriate; a birthday card signed by the researchers she supported *is* appropriate and will be displayed for months.

Photos of buildings being built, people at work fulfill-ing the mission, thank-you notes from board members and senior staff are not only inexpensive – they will be treasured mementoes from your organization. We can never underestimate the power of a simple thank-you note. Write them often and write them with genuine words of appreciation. When I suggest "write them," I sincerely mean to hand write them on simple thank-you cards. If your organization has blank cards use them, but inexpensive thank-you notes with your business card inserted are truly appreciated, especially by our older donors.

Today's stewardship, or "impact" report, is likely the best example of providing meaningful communication to a donor on an annual basis. It isn't necessary to make the reports complex or expensive – the most important thing to do with all forms of stewardship is to simply do it! If a report contains a thank-you letter from your most senior volunteer or leader, two or three pages of actual accomplishments with information about the people that benefit from your mission activities and what you are doing to achieve your vision, you will have a stewardship report that a donor will read (and likely share with a friend) and remember.

The "seven times rule" of thanking a donor is at least thirty years old – it's time to make stewardship reports the new rule.

After recently attending a number of philanthropic conferences in Canada and the US, I know that stewardship reports and better stewardship activities are golden – we need to ensure that stewardship reports become true "best practice" – the way we know prospect research is critical to securing a gift in the first place. I have never had a donor indicate that they would stop their pledge because the report was inappropriate or late. I have heard first-hand, coupled with stories from colleagues, that the stewardship report is *critical* to major gift success.

Within our sector, it is common knowledge that people move on to other organizations and are promoted frequently if they have the 4 nonprofit "E's" – education, experience, ethics and excellent work. So, why have we not figured out a way to help our charities raise more funds and protect our donor's commitment to our mission, after working so hard to secure their trust, faith in our vision and increasingly important funds? Why do we continuously fall down and ignore donors after they have made major gift commitments?

MY SOLUTION

Just like writing a Case for Support, there is a formula or solution to the problems that organizations face when it comes to stewardship. I believe that all non-profit employees should detail (in writing) important donor information before moving to another charity. Even without a donor wall or annual honour roll in the annual report, at least three people in the charity (even if volunteers!) should have up-to-date information so that stewardship can be conducted.

The disappointed donors (*imagine how many people they tell when they stop their pledge payments!*) that aren't stewarded in-between pledge payments require twice as much time and effort (equal to donor dollars) to regain trust and the possible renewal of their gift.

When I think back to the look exchanged between that lovely and generous couple on that fateful tour, I credit them with making me a better steward and increasingly zealous about teaching best practice. Even if you pick up the phone five times a week and call a donor just to say hello and thanks, it will make a difference. If each of your board members were to do it, plus a few volunteers and each staff person; it would add up to a lot of good will for your organization. Do it, not just because stewardship works and it is becoming increasingly important – but, because it is a core value in our profession. It is just the right thing to do when someone gives you a gift.

THE VIGILANT FUNDRAISER

STEP

5

FUNDRAISING
COMMITTEE

---

*"Fundraising is a
team sport!"*

A word from George...

I can understand how it happens. Board members are recruited for their leadership potential or for their affiliation with a key corporate partner or because an individual expresses an interest in being more involved with your charity. The reflex of the charity is to say "yes" to <u>availability,</u> not assess for <u>ability.</u> As a result, your organization may have a board that is not going to be much help with your fundraising efforts. The vigilant fundraiser knows not to accept this as status quo. Instead, consider forming a fundraising or development committee that may include some board members but can also be sourced from a bigger network of contacts.

Your fund development committee becomes your fundraising "champions." With the right training (see Step 6) these volunteers will lead your campaigns, support staff initiatives and rally even more volunteer support to your cause. But, it starts here — by identifying appropriate candidates and developing your committee through the use of a structured system and tools.

***Lee Pigeau** is an experienced fundraiser and teacher who, in Step 5, will take you through the mechanics of building your committee. There is no need for the vigilant fundraiser to "go it alone." The greatest success in fundraising will be found when you approach it as a team sport.*

DEVELOP A FUNDRAISING COMMITTEE

BY LEE PIGEAU

Charities, almost by definition raise funds to some extent or another. For many charities, the funds raised through donations, events and "drives" are the only money that the organization has to fund its good work. Because fundraising is so integral to the health of a charity, planning and implementation has to start at the top — with the board and senior management. Fundraising is a team sport and the establishment of a permanent fundraising team (not an ad hoc committee) is essential to success.

A VIGILANT FUNDRAISER ACTIVELY RECRUITS THE SKILLS THAT ARE NEEDED

This is perhaps the most dramatic shift from past practice — moving towards recruitment of volunteers, as you would recruit paid workers. We want to hire for skills, instead of taking the first warm body to walk through the door to fill a position, or scrambling to find something — anything — for a volunteer to do to keep them busy. We want to create a job description for a certain task and recruit for skills related to that task.

If you want to attract and keep good volunteers for your organization, you're going to have to create a program that recognizes what it is that motivates volunteers, and design positions that are desirable. Volunteers are too busy and too demanding – and there are too many other choices for them out there.

Recruiting a fundraising committee is important, but how do you find them and recruit them to become your champions? Who are the best people to work on this team?

The simplest answer to these questions is: people who understand your mission and priorities and enjoy asking for money! However, those individuals are the exception and not the rule; therefore, the following information should help develop your committee.

COMMITTEE DEVELOPMENT

Considering that the financial health of a charity is a fundamental board responsibility then the logical place to start is with board members. Ideally, board members are highly engaged and set an example for others throughout the organization to follow. A good fundraising committee focuses on establishing and building lasting relationships with donors as a shared responsibility throughout your organization not just fundraising and administrative staff. Everyone must understand that they play an important part in fundraising success, regardless of their position.

A fundraising or development committee takes on a leadership role for planning and implementing revenue-generating strategies. Often a member of the board chairs the committee but ideally, community members who are not on the board are members too. In fact, your fundraising committee can be a brilliant "tryout" for future board members and an effective introduction into your organization's culture.

The fundraising committee has basic responsibility for overseeing, advising and with staff, implementing the organization's fundraising activities. Its main duties are to:

- *Set policies, priorities, and goals for fundraising programs for the current fiscal year.*
- *Review the ongoing performance of each campaign.*
- *Review campaign achievement versus its objectives.*
- *Identify and rate all major prospects for support.*
- *Recruit key volunteer leaders and solicitors for the organization's fundraising campaigns.*
- *Be an active part of fundraising for the organization.*

Chairs of development committees, like development directors, meet the income needs of the organization without exhausting its base of support. The best development committee chairpersons are able to see the job in its entirety. They have broad vision. They don't fall in love with one fundraising idea, event, or concept at the expense of the overall development effort.

TERMS OF REFERENCE

Thriving committees work within rules established by written Terms of Reference or a Memorandum of Understanding. This statement or description will clearly set out expectations to volunteers and staff of what the commitment is and what contribution each person will make to the organization. These terms ensure that everyone knows what is expected of him or her and what impact they will have on the team.

Subjects or headings within these guidelines may include:

Structure and purpose: How many people are on the committee; the hierarchy and reporting structure as well as the reason the committee exists.

Duties, roles and responsibilities: Detail what the committee does and does not do in relation to tasks, targets and timelines. This can also include decision-making protocol or authority, finances and committee budget.

Internal support: Staff / volunteer connections as well as budget or resources the committee has at its disposal.

Meetings: Honestly outline the timing, length and content of what happens when the committee gets together.

Terms of office: This is probably the most important piece; describing what each individual committee member is expected to do.

Sub-committees: Sub-committees allow for even further expansion of the volunteer program by creating special teams for specific purposes: such as special events, major gifts, monthly donors' gift club, stewardship and capital campaigns.

Fundraising activities or deliverables: List the activities and actions for the team and everything the charity does to raise funds.

Qualifications / experience: Outline the expertise, background and connections the volunteers should bring to the committee.

Benefits of membership: Tell what is in it for your volunteers. Are there any professional development opportunities or other types of training?

Dispute resolution: This is rarely done, but very helpful if and when a disagreement occurs.

The bottom line is that the clearer your document, the less room there is for misunderstanding or unmet expectations.

It is also important to have a volunteer job description. Again, the purpose of this document is to be as honest as possible about what the understanding is between the charity and its volunteers and staff. The goal is to clarify what is often unspoken; preferably before the volunteer commits or an issue arises. In order to be effective, you need to provide the potential volunteer with a position description that will speak to their motivations, and give them a clear understanding of what the job requires – for example:

- *Job title*
- *Objectives*
- *Qualifications*
- *Responsibilities*
- *Orientation and training*
- *Commitment – time and place*

A volunteer should also receive (in writing) details regarding the benefits and skills development that they will receive from the position. They need to know that they will be supported in their work, and that they will derive some intrinsic benefits for their time and effort. A comprehensive position description will be your most effective recruitment tool.

You'll note that this sounds a great deal like the terms of reference, but each member of the committee and sub-committee has a different part to play.

THE VOLUNTEER APPLICATION FORM
AND AGREEMENTS

A volunteer application will provide you with the necessary background information needed to have the volunteer begin assisting your organization. Every volunteer must fill out the information on the form as part of the screening process. Far too often, organizations are so thankful to get a helper that they often overlook screening unsuitable candidates. Applications are another opportunity to reinforce the charity's expectations before you recruit the wrong individual.

Screening occurs through a full police check, calling references, identifying previous volunteer experience, expectations, etc. The volunteer application should have basic contact information (both home and business), education, current and previous employment experience, other volunteering and service clubs, special skills and should ask questions about what the volunteer would like to do, and their availability to do so. Requesting that a resume be attached is good too. The application form allows fundraising staff to leverage connections the volunteer may have, even though the volunteer may not be aware of the benefits of involvement in such things as service clubs and alumni associations.

Also essential is an agreement between the charity and volunteer that will include information about your charity's values and expectations for behaviour. Confidentiality and waiver of liability are fundamental parts of this agreement. One especially important part of this agreement for fundraising volunteers clarifies that volunteers are not to be making their own sales pitches or using your prospect research for their own benefit.

WHAT TYPE OF PERSON SHOULD BE ON THE FUNDRAISING COMMITTEE?

Generally, the type of people who are comfortable asking for funds are more extroverted than introverted. That said, quiet and reflective individuals also play a vital role in fundraising. They are often better researchers or listeners than their more outgoing counterparts. Paired together on a request for support, it is easy to see how they can be a formidable team. One learns about the prospect's interests and preferences while the other makes the pitch asking for the gift.

So although we are trying to anticipate who our ideal volunteer might be for a specific position, don't be too restrictive. Be creative – and really, don't wander too far from home. In fundraising, your most committed supporter, your closest "family" members are the most likely to help you out.

Fundraising can take a lot of preparation and a certain amount of tenacity. Think about who has experience "closing deals." Often times, business people with a sales or marketing background will prefer asking prospective donors directly for a gift than they will attending a fundraising event or cooking for a bake sale. Conversely, there are a number of individuals who would much rather volunteer at a charity gala than make a face-to-face request.

Be sure to ask people what types of tasks they enjoy doing, or want to learn when you are creating your team. While it may seem obvious, having an avid golfer as your Golf Committee Chair is important. It means they will be more interested in the event and won't need training on hole-in-one contests and scoring. Special event sub-committees are great places for people with a passion for their hobbies and your organization.

Characteristics of a good fundraising committee member:
- *Commitment to your charity's mission and values*
- *Commitment to follow best practices in fundraising*
- *Knowledge of the local community*
- *Strong leadership, delegation, and communication skills*
- *Respect and understanding of the roles of volunteers and staff in the volunteer/staff partnership*
- *Time management and organizational skills*
- *Action and results-oriented*
- *Is a donor to your organization*

WHERE TO FIND POTENTIAL COMMITTEE MEMBERS?

Once you have outlined your committee expecta-tions and developed the necessary documentation to ensure clear communication, get the word out in your community. Start internally by recruiting the friends and families of your existing staff and volunteers. Consider contacting service clubs and local churches. Check your newspaper and radio outlets to see if they offer any public service announcements.

Never underestimate the value of the fundraising training that your local hospital, college, or United Way provides to their campaign canvassers. If there has been a significant capital campaign for funds in your community, research the volunteers who were involved. While they may not agree to sit on your committee right away, they usually have acquired valuable skills that will remain with them. Does anyone in your organization have a personal contact with him or her? *This is a great time to pull out the volunteer application form to note connections.* If so, do they know the candidate well enough to comment on their interest in your mission? It is always helpful to cultivate these community leaders and nurture a relationship as a donor or volunteer.

Donors make great volunteers! They have already demonstrated their commitment to your organization by investing funds. If time permits, they may be interested in helping even further. Be sure to acknowledge their generosity before asking them, just like you should recognize a volunteer's time prior to soliciting funds. It's important to show respect and gratitude for their current contributions. Even when donors can't commit to sit on a fundraising committee, they may know a family member, employee or friend who can.

Corporate donors, especially those who sponsor community events almost always want to show commitment with their people as well as their money. Recruiting committee members from major sponsors for events and as solicitors for funds from other companies in the same industry can be a way for your business champions to showcase their corporate responsibility – for the benefit of your charity.

TRAINING

Provide your committee members with the necessary training they need to do an effective job. Step 6 will outline the best practices in this regard. While some unique individuals may be naturals at asking for money, it's unlikely for most. Help your volunteers understand best practices, give them opportunities to role-play and try out a scripted request to strengthen their abilities.

Over and over again, consultants hear that once volunteers are recruited, they receive no guidance or information. If your volunteers are going to continue the volunteer cycle and help you to recruit others, it is important that they are happy.

Don't forget to provide your fundraising committee members with feedback. One of the reasons that terms of reference and job descriptions are used during recruitment is to strengthen the chances of success.

Use these recruitment tools to make the volunteer's experience better and provide your organization with more impact. Give people the opportunity to grow to new levels by reinforcing positive outcomes or identifying areas for improvement.

DON'T FORGET TO SAY "THANK-YOU" IN A VARIETY OF WAYS

Help your volunteer feel like "one of the family" and at home in your organization. You might consider welcoming them with a coffee mug that they know they'll find when they arrive at your office. Include all volunteers in holiday gatherings, and send a brief handwritten note or perhaps a birthday card to recognize special occasions. Thank-you gestures can be small and inexpensive or free tokens of gratitude that help ensure an ongoing relationship. Just as we need to steward our donors, a vigilant fundraiser should do the same to strengthen the bond with your organization's volunteers.

One of the most powerful ways to thank a fundraising committee member is to show them the impact that their efforts have made on your charity. Tell them what their time and effort bought! If a committee raised funds that enabled you to buy new equipment, show them the equipment being used. If fundraising helped start a program, bring in a client to tell what the program has done for them.

It's a simple thing to make people feel good about their contribution of time, talent, and in some cases, treasure. You will be pleasantly rewarded by their willingness to lend a hand again the next time you ask.

THE VIGILANT FUNDRAISER

STEP

TRAIN
VOLUNTEERS

---

*"The consequence of not
training is not being able to
recruit quality volunteers."*

A word from George...

I talk a lot about "cause and effect" and the need for a vigilant fundraiser to constantly revisit each step of the fundraising process looking for areas of improvement and alignment.

In Step 5 we address the need for a dedicated and focused fundraising committee, recruited with intent and clear expectations. Now in Step 6 we focus on the training of those volunteers who are becoming advocates for your charity out in the community.

The training of volunteers is an investment by the organization being made to ensure the success of its various fundraising initiatives. It's a win-win-win proposition. First of all, the volunteers <u>want to be trained</u> and are waiting for your direction and teaching. Secondly, a teaching environment provides positive modeling for both volunteers and staff where the sharing of best-practices is both encouraged and valued. Finally, (and I can't stress this enough) the better the training of the volunteer, the more dollars will be raised for you and your organization.

The consequence of not providing adequate training is not being able to recruit quality volunteers and as a result, raising less money for your cause.

*In Step 6, **Lee Pigeau** gives you step-by-step instructions on how to train those valuable volunteers you have worked so hard to recruit to your campaign. Vigilant fundraisers, pay attention to the details, they matter!*

TRAIN VOLUNTEERS ON "MAKING THE ASK"

BY LEE PIGEAU

Asking for money is the single most important function of a fundraising volunteer, but it is also one of the most stress-inducing and difficult tasks for a volunteer who is not fully prepared. Many capable people find soliciting gifts extremely difficult and even embarrassing. Because of this, every charity should make training fundraising volunteers a special priority.

Volunteers who are comfortable, motivated and confident get the biggest gifts in any campaign. Whether your volunteers have been with your organization for a long time or are newly recruited, it is important that everyone has the same understanding of how to "make the ask."

While education should be ongoing, it is essential that a formal training session be held before every campaign effort, and for each new volunteer.

The session should cover every aspect of the solicitation

process, including:

- *where to conduct the meeting*
- *how much to request*
- *who should be involved*
- *how much time should be spent*

You should offer suggestions on how to deal with prospects who are reluctant to meet, as well as the "art" of leaving the donor with a positive feeling when the gift received falls below the solicitor's expectations.

Ordinarily, a training meeting lasts two hours and provides an atmosphere that is encouraging and flexible to the skills and temperament of your volunteers.

The essence of successful face-to-face fundraising is having "the right person ask the right person for the right amount at the right time." The right solicitor always starts from a perspective of personal dedication and enthusiasm for the charity and its future plans. Your training should reflect this.

WHAT DO VOLUNTEERS NEED TO KNOW?

Provide organization-specific information that your volunteers can use when out in the field: your Case for Support, FAQs on your charity as well as testimonials and/or stories about who or what you support. Information on recognition opportunities and the benefits to donating to the specific campaign or project must also be given to each volunteer. A manual that has all of this information as well as the tips below is a welcome addition for most volunteers

Help your volunteer set the stage. Preparation is essential. Give them the tools they need to know about the prospective donor, where and when to set up a meeting and, when necessary, how to cultivate the prospect over a series of meetings and events. The circumstances and conditions in which a solicitation visit takes place can affect its outcome. The following suggestions will help your volunteers get on the right track.

•*Start scheduling solicitation visits* within a day or two after attending the orientation and training meeting and after carefully reviewing the solicitation materials.

•*Schedule solicitation meetings in advance.* Don't surprise your prospect. Make solicitation visits in teams of two whenever possible. Two volunteers or a staff member and a volunteer together can build confidence and can emphasize the importance of the visit to the prospective donor.

•*When making a team visit,* decide in advance who will – make the appointment; open the discussion; ask for the commitment and bring the meeting to a close. Review your approach. Try to anticipate possible questions and concerns, and be prepared to answer in a positive way. Conducting role-play at the training session will often increase confidence for the actual visit.

- *Meet when it is most comfortable* for the prospect. For individuals, this will usually be at their home in the evening or on the weekend. For businesses, early in the morning or during a natural "down time" is best.

- *Allow 45 minutes or more* for an effective visit and presentation.

- *Be friendly and sociable* but keep to the purpose for being there.

Volunteers should be encouraged to find out as much as they can about their prospective donor before the visit; specific aspects of the Case for Support might appeal more to your prospective donor than others. Providing this information in a confidential briefing can make all the difference to the confidence of the volunteer and the success of the ask.

SCHEDULING THE FACE-TO-FACE MEETING

Scheduling the face-to-face meeting can be a difficult task. Prepare your volunteers with tips such as:

- *Start off a phone call* in a conversational tone, a "How are you" type conversation. A good way to swing into the "meat" of the call is to simply state it:

    "{Name of Prospect}, the reason I'm calling you is to see when we could get together for an hour or so to discuss a subject that is very close to me, and I think

> *to you as well {name of organization}. Would you*
> *have an hour this week when we could meet?"*

•*Remember, the purpose of telephoning is to "sell"* the personal visit, not to discuss donation levels. A common mistake is to be drawn into making the ask over the phone, which normally yields poorer results.

•*Comments from the prospective donor* such as, "What's it all about?" or "I really can't afford to give very much right now" can be turned around to help confirm the appointment. A good response could be:

> *"That's one of the points that I'd like to discuss*
> *when we get together. Is there an hour this week you*
> *could set aside to see me?"*

•*Respectful persistence* almost always nets a positive result.

INSTRUCTION ON HOW TO "MAKE THE ASK"

Helping your volunteers complete the ask is a critical aspect of the solicitation. Tips should include: the importance of preparation, asking for a specific amount and how to set the stage during the meeting.

•*To help the volunteer relax,* tell them it is OK to enter into casual conversation until they are comfortable. A good way to start a conversation is to talk about common interests. Suggest that they introduce themselves as being part of a special group undertaking some select donor visits on behalf of the charity.

- *Remind them of the importance of being a good listener.* Allowing the prospective donor an opportunity to talk may give the volunteer a sense of what particular aspects of the Case for Support may or may not appeal to them. Also, many people, when they are comfortable with the purpose of the visit, will voluntarily begin discussing their business and financial affairs.

- *Urge volunteers to (whenever possible) take their time!* Do not rush a visit. Remind the volunteers that they are helping a prospective donor to make the financial decision to support the campaign.

- *Instruct volunteers to use the materials provided* to them to inform the prospective donor of the wonderful work that the charity does, and how the funds will benefit the community. Emphasize those aspects of the case that the volunteer believes will have the greatest appeal to the particular prospect. It is important that the appeal be personal and positive at all times. It would be unwise to say:

    "{Name of Prospect}, you may not be interested in this, but ..." It will be effective to say: "{Name of Prospect}, I am convinced of the tremendous need for this, and I hope you agree ...!"

- *The rationale for supporting the campaign* should be

presented in a way that is natural for both the volunteer and the prospect. Have the volunteer tell the story in their own words. Encourage them to talk about the reasons they are involved – why they personally are investing their time and money.

• *Keeping the conversation on track.* This is where a partner can really help. It is also helpful to instruct your volunteers to keep the solicitation materials in front of the prospective donor at all times. Role-play and practice can be of benefit here as well.

REQUESTING A GIFT

In the training session it is important to go over the specifics of requesting a gift.

Provide your volunteers with a sample script that outlines the ideal scenarios. This occurs when, after reviewing the materials the prospective donor indicates that s/he is interested in the campaign and is willing to contribute. At this point, it is essential that the volunteer asks for a specific amount. For example:

> *"{Name of prospect}, we are asking people in situations that appear similar to yours to consider a gift of $_____."*

• *Tell your volunteers that the prospective donors must be given time to react.* Remind them to take a breath or a sip of coffee before speaking again.

• *As a means of enhancing the possibilities* of receiving the requested gift, a volunteer can talk about donor recognition opportunities.

• *The rationale behind the amount requested* must be familiar to the volunteer. They can discuss the importance of receiving the requested gift amount. If possible, give examples of what the gift will accomplish. It may be good to mention in passing that the gift benefits the prospective donor's income tax. This should not be stressed though, since the prospective donor's motivation is to support the charity.

THE DONOR RESPONDS

Practice how to manage the response of the donor. The volunteer needs to be prepared to hear "yes," or "yes to a lower amount," a "maybe" or even a "no." Your volunteer fundraisers need to have the ability to respectfully negotiate these circumstances and ethically respond to the donor's response to the request for funds. It's a fine line. An overly-enthusiastic volunteer can lose a gift because of a demanding attitude. Because of this, the training session must outline what a volunteer should do in the following circumstances.

THE PROSPECTIVE DONOR REQUESTS TIME
TO CONSIDER THE REQUEST

This should be seen as a positive sign that the volunteer has been accurate with the request. The prospective donor may wish to consider the matter further and discuss it with family members, business associates, accountants, etc. Additional time should be granted and appreciation shown for the willingness to give the request further consideration. The next step will be for the visitor to secure a follow-up appointment scheduled not later than ten days after the initial meeting. The objective is to receive an answer to the request in a personal interview rather than through the mail or over the telephone. Remind your volunteers not to leave the letter of intent behind.

THE PROSPECTIVE DONOR AGREES
TO THE REQUEST

Tell your volunteers not to prolong the visit at this point because many people have experienced a change of mind when "oversold." Volunteers should be instructed on how to suggest that the donor fill out the letter of intent or prepare a short letter stating their intentions. The total amount of the gift and the method of payment should be clearly indicated.

THE PROSPECTIVE DONOR
HAS OBJECTIONS OR QUESTIONS

While almost all volunteers are liable to get objections at some point, remind them to keep them in perspective. *An objection is not a "no."* It is simply a request for more information and should be treated as such. Ask your volunteer fundraiser to encourage the prospect to convey the things that are important to her / him about the organization / project. Try responding with the "Feel, Felt, Found" method:

> *"{Name of prospect}, I know just how you feel.*
> *Many of our donors have felt the pressure to give more*
> *this year. But what I have found was that the increase*
> *in community need required that they re-evaluate*
> *their philanthropic investments this year."*

Train volunteers on how to answer questions. It is vitally important to practice answering questions, especially questions that you know will come up in conversation. Role-play between staff and experienced and confident volunteers in the training session can help everyone be comfortable with the notion that questions are not challenges, but opportunities to further advance the cause. However, give your volunteers permission to say "I don't know, but I'll get back to you tomorrow with the answer." Remind them that in these cases follow-up is the *only way* they will be successful.

THE PROSPECTIVE DONOR SAYS "NO"

It is a basic principle of successful fundraising to always leave the door open for future possibilities. Therefore, your volunteers must be explicitly reminded that it is important to avoid any confrontational situations. Insist that they avoid expressing anger or impatience when the prospective donor has refused to make a gift. Suggest the possibility of a future gift as a viable option.

A well-trained and confident volunteer may be able to determine why the request was refused, so that in the future the same pitfalls can be avoided. A polite request for a reason is almost never turned down and getting this information can be enlightening for other volunteers if it points out weaknesses in the case, process or project.

Volunteers need to be reminded that they are asking for a *gift* and it is the prospective donor's right to say no. Very valid and personal reasons for a refusal, that were previously unknown, are common and respect is important.

AN ATTITUDE OF GRATITUDE

In all donor visits instruct volunteer fundraisers to express gratitude for being given the time to discuss the charity. Leave the prospective donor with a suggestion to think about the charity in the weeks ahead. Politely end the visit.

Instruct them on what to do after the visit. Post-meeting, volunteers must thank the donor in writing for their time and follow up on any questions, concerns and, hopefully, promises that were expressed.

Instructing volunteers on the importance of detailed feedback is essential to the success of your current campaign and future projects involving the donor and the volunteer. Being able to celebrate success, follow-up on requests or to refocus on other efforts all stems from knowing what happened on the call.

Provide your volunteers with a feedback form that they can send to the office to be entered into a database and used for follow-up and future reference. The feedback form can also provide tips and reminders on how to thank a prospective donor after the visit. In the case of a joint visit with a staff member and volunteer, it is all too easy for this task to be delegated to the person getting paid. The perspective of the volunteer is extremely important and their buy-in throughout the entire process will make everyone's job smoother.

While a training session at the beginning of the process is the most formal and detailed way to train volunteers, it is not the end of the learning process.

Have your volunteers meet on a regular basis and share their experiences so that others can learn from them. Celebrating success as a group is a great motivator. Acknowledging disappointments and visits that were not successful helps to mitigate any bad feelings, and provides learning opportunities for the group.

As the campaign or project proceeds, providing ongoing feedback on what is and isn't working, will make each visit, event and opportunity more fruitful and give your volunteer fundraisers the information and confidence they need for a successful experience.

STEP

7

IDENTIFY KEY
STAKEHOLDERS

---

*"...an Excel spreadsheet
is not a database!"*

A word from George...

*At first glance, Step 7 may seem very straight forward; identify your stakeholders and target audiences. However, what we find at the heart of identifying your stakeholders is... a database. I know that no one wants to talk data. As **Liz Rejman** says in our next chapter, "database management is like the foundation for a house — structurally essential, but not particularly glamorous."*

But consider how important accurate lists are for the vigilant fundraiser. How many of these groups do you communicate with?

- *Volunteers and Staff*
- *Donors*
- *Service Clubs*
- *Foundations*
- *Corporate*
- *Media*
- *Politicians (federal, provincial, municipal)*

What kind of resource are you currently using? Can it be improved upon? Remember that an Excel spreadsheet is not a database! At a minimum, centralizing your sources of information is a place to start so that fundraising opportunities are not thwarted due to mishandled information resulting in poor stewardship.

In Step 9 we explore communication in greater detail but suffice to say that many communication efforts fail because they target everyone. In reality, most outreach should target a specific group of people. Having a functional database allows a vigilant fundraiser to focus messaging, resources and strategy where it counts.

As you read Liz's on-target advice for managing your data and identifying key stakeholders, I offer you two challenges:

Name your "wish list" If you could convince 130 people to embrace your message today who would they be? Why? What can they do for you? What do they think about your issue now? What are the key things they need to believe to help you? How can you better focus on influencing this target audience?

Draw your target circle Before beginning any outreach efforts you need to accurately draw some target circles of influence around your audience. Who is in the centre? What is the message they need to understand? What is the action they need to take? Each ring around the circle symbolizes an audience that can help you reach the target audience.

THE VIGILANT FUNDRAISER

IDENTIFY YOUR
KEY STAKEHOLDERS

BY LIZ REJMAN

Are you able to easily produce an accurate list of your key stakeholders, your most loyal donors and your best prospects? I don't mean the list you mentally keep track of and rhyme off based on anecdotal evidence; I mean a list of key constituents based on a set of quantitative criteria and characteristics that anyone in the organization can recreate at any moment in time. And does that list contain accurate biographical information, giving history, past interactions and future intentions? Or do you need to reference paper files and staff member's memories?

Essentially, what is the status of your data?

We live in an age of personalization and customization. Gone are the days when unaddressed solicitations and thank-you form letters are acceptable to donors. Failure to know and understand your key stakeholders (present and future) hampers your ability to meet and exceed the goals of your organization. The collection and analysis of data provides us with the chance to optimize opportunities, exploit cost-saving measures and provides us with the ability to make decisions based on quantifiable information.

DATA MANAGEMENT

So are you collecting, tracking and monitoring data about your key stakeholders on a regular basis? Is data management important in your organization? Or are you relying on spreadsheets and institutional memory to help you generate your future funding?

Let's face it: database management is like the foundation for a house – structurally essential, but not particularly glamorous. It requires careful consideration and significant investment as does any infrastructure but no one necessarily coos over it. It isn't as fun as engaging with donors on social media channels, and it doesn't excite or move people as much as great copy or beautiful graphics.

Just as hope is not a strategy, an Excel spreadsheet is not a database. It's true that from the perspective of the Canada Revenue Agency, an excel spreadsheet will fulfill all required obligations. But you are doing your organization a disservice, and stunting the growth potential of gifts, with this short-sighted tactic.

Your database should be your organization's memory centre. It must include, at the very minimum–

- *biographical information;*
- *giving history;*
- *event attendance;*
- *board membership; and*
- *unique communications between your organization and its constituents.*

Donors and volunteers enter relationships with your organization and as such, the organization has an obligation to ensure an accurate and complete recording is maintained of that relationship. In effect, your database should be the single source of truth for your organization. Should anyone ask – they should be able to find the answers in your database. And an Excel spreadsheet isn't going to effectively manage such an important and complex task.

DATA MAINTENANCE

Like the foundation of your home, you must carefully consider what material is used and how it is structured. An essential question your organization should ask itself is: Do we have an A.C.E. database? That is, does your database contain *accurate information* with *consistent coding* that allows for the *efficient* use of the data? Inaccurate information coupled with inconsistent coding results in the manual handling of data – a recipe for human error resulting in costly mistakes. Therefore, you must think of a database as a dynamic structure, it requires attention and adjustment on an ongoing basis. Your efforts should be focused on the maintenance of the data, rather than in the manual manipulation of the data. This effort results in data that is accurate, consistent and efficiently segmented.

While a database should be viewed as the historical memory of your organization, the data contained within the system informs decisions. Data uncovers future key stakeholders such as your potential major giving donors, your planned giving prospects or your ideal demographic to solicit in an acquisition mailing. Many fundraising organizations seem to think that the answer to future funding lies in the external. In fact, the answer is to be found internally within your own data.

It is far less expensive to engage with existing donors than acquire new ones. For example, planned giving donors are your frequent, faithful annual fund donors. They are the constituents who give consistently, regardless of dollar amount, year after year for multiple years. Major giving prospects are constituents that have a capacity to give generously and have either an affinity or connection to your organization. In terms of acquisition solicitations, you need to understand the characteristics of your typical donor in order to target similar constituents. All of this information should be in your database.

PRINCIPLES OF DATA COLLECTION

In order to utilize your data to its greatest potential, there must be a systematic collection and extraction of data fields. So, how is that accomplished? Here are 10 principles that any organization regardless of the type of database they have, needs to incorporate for effective data management:

1. *Everyone in your organization is accountable for the integrity of the data. No exceptions. This doesn't mean that everyone in your organization needs to be proficient at updating the database themselves, but they need to understand they are responsible for informing someone in your organization as soon as possible when a change in data is required.*

2. *Think with the end in mind. What information do you need to speak with credibility and transparency to your donors, volunteers and stakeholders? What reports do you want to generate and how do you want them to look? It is easier to decide coding conventions and determine what data is important if you know how it will be used and for what purpose.*

3. *Inspire enthusiasm for data entry. If people don't understand the importance of data management and how it can help them, they will not support the ongoing efforts of data collection and will view it as an annoyance.*

4. *Collect data that will help you further understand*

*your target audience. Specifically, look to populate
information on affinity, wealth indicators, and
connections, but know that any and all information
that positively moves a relationship with a prospect
forward should be collected, recorded and reviewed.*

5. *Establish coding conventions and a common internal
language. Appoint a data cop to enforce these
conventions and train staff on why and how to
input and update information into the database.*

6. *Gather data in fields, not in free form text. It is
much easier to query and extract data that is
consistent in format; otherwise, you will always
be manually manipulating data rather than
analyzing data.*

7. *Add and edit information in your database on an
ongoing basis. There will never be a good time to
update information.*

8. *Review data conventions and coding on a scheduled
basis. Mistakes happen, ensure that you are not
missing opportunities due to improper coding. It
is easier and less stressful to clean-up data on a
scheduled basis, rather than immediately before
an important mailing or meeting.*

9. *Generate reports on a consistent basis. Timing is
important when engaging with your stakeholders
and target audiences, reviewing reports regularly
will help you spot the opportunities to engage and*

connect with your constituents.

10. *Data is dynamic and ever-changing, as are your programs, goals and personnel. Be flexible with the notion that report formats will change, the importance of certain data sets will vary and there will <u>always</u> be new information to collect.*

Data is your organization's foundation. Are you standing on shaky or solid ground when it comes to data management? Do you have data intelligence that is accurate, consistent and efficient which will empower your organization? Or are bad data habits crippling your efforts? Make sure you can define and identify your stakeholders and target audiences so that you can focus your message, resources and strategy where it counts.

TIP: Conduct an RFM analysis
of your current donors

Conducting a simple RFM analysis on the individuals who have given philanthropically to your organization is an easy and simple way to determine the top 20% of donors to your organization.

RFM stands for Recency, Frequency, and Monetary and is a form of in-house analysis originally conducted by corporate sales teams to sleuth out their best customers. Essentially it is a quantifiable way of determining the donors who have given most recently, who give most frequently and who give most generously. Find the donors who are within the top 20% of each of those categories, and you have found your best donors to nurture, steward and invite as your next set of key stakeholders.

STEP

PLANNED
GIVING

---

*"Planned gifts put the power
of philanthropy back into the hands
of the middle class."*

A word from George...

Here's why the vigilant fundraiser will include planned giving as part of their development strategy.

As a fresh young fundraiser I approached an older donor to make a pledge. The ask was for $5,000 a year over five years. His reply was this — "George, I don't even buy green bananas anymore."

There are many points of view around the need for planned gifts and the ways in which we, as fundraisers, approach and talk about them. Whether you choose to refer to it as planned giving, a bequest program or legacy program — it is simply the name applied to a program to inspire donors to establish tax-wise gifts of support through their financial and estate plan.

For me, the bottom line is that a planned giving program doesn't have to be sophisticated but adopting a proactive approach to this area of fundraising will ensure that you are being vigilant and responsive to the needs of your donors. My donor who wouldn't buy green bananas may have been a perfect candidate for a legacy gift even if it wasn't explicitly stated. You will also meet donors who say that they "wish there was more they could do." This is a clear expression of philanthropic desire that will open the door for a planned giving discussion.

*There is no bigger advocate for adopting legacy giving into your fundraising strategy than **Paul Nazareth**. His enthusiasm and spirit for Step 8 of the fundraising process embodies all that comes with being a vigilant fundraiser.*

PLANNED GIVING:
THE PHILANTHROPIC
PHILOSOPHER'S STONE

BY PAUL NAZARETH

If I had one beef with the common assumption fellow fundraisers have about "planned giving" peers it's that planned giving fundraisers are tax-sorcerers and mathematical magicians. Herb Gale of the Presbyterian Church and Jeff Pym of the Waterloo Seminary College at Laurier gave a wonderful seminar at a *Canadian Association of Gift Planners'* annual conference that touched on this strategic misnomer. They gave the audience a history of the "philosopher's stone," the element sought for centuries that would help turn useless lead into gold. It was also sometimes believed to be an elixir of life, useful for rejuvenation and possibly for achieving immortality. *Much like legacy philanthropy is often described.*

> *It's not magic.*
> **Desire to Give + Tax and Estate Planning =**
> **Legacy Philanthropy.**
> *Period.*

Today there are college, university, Masters and MBA programs in fundraising and philanthropy. When I started my career in fundraising my only experience was being a life-long volunteer who excelled at raising money. But I had one clear personal bias – I really didn't and still don't like the fundraising machine. Direct mail, the calls at home, solicitors stopping me on the sidewalk, the constant barrage of emails for friends walking, swimming, growing and shaving hair for a cure, the cause, our community; at times it's a bit much.

Fundraising boards are always chasing new shiny things; like Facebook giving pages, text donations and the power of Crowdfunding. It's that age-old argument that if we "all gave one dollar..." or "cut out our daily coffee" we could change the world. I get it. You hold a box of chocolate almonds in your hand and you sell it for money or you tap your network to sponsor you or buy a lottery ticket for a worthwhile cause. It seems so simple. Even at the major gift level, the pressure of campaigns and fiscal year-ends is so artificial and out of step with the open conversation with a donor I thought, this is just not going to work. Also, I need my daily coffee or someone is going to get hurt.

THE CHILDREN ARE NOT OUR FUTURE

Ask yourself these questions.

  1. *Who actually has the disposable social capital?*

2. *Who has been giving over a lifetime, is educated in the mission enough to make a thoughtful gift?*

3. *Who cares about the cause and organization the most?*

A young person can make (at best) an annual gift, but they have just met the charity. A 70-year-old has engaged this cause longer than a 20-year-old has been alive. The dollar value of a planned gift is 1000 times a donor's annual gift. When asked, the average Canadian says they would make a significant gift to charity if they won the lottery. Well, to put it all out there, death is the lottery and everybody wins! (Maybe don't put that in your next brochure).

Canada has the most generous bequest tax treatments in the developed world. If everything you own on earth is considered income when you die and you will of course pay income tax on that amount, *but* you're allowed to give away 100% of that taxed amount to charity. Who wouldn't do that?!

THE POWER OF PLANNED GIFTS

Planned giving is the democratization of philanthropy, which is often forced to focus on the wealthy. Gala dinners and patron-style giving is begging at the table. Planned gifts put the power of philanthropy back into the hands of the middle class. Any older couple with grown children or no children who own their own home will probably have an estate worth six or seven figures, a large demographic part of the population can make this gift.

As a planned giving-focused fundraiser, I have met some of the most humble, kind, and thoughtful people in the world. They care most about saving lives and having impact instead of aggressively negotiating to have their names on buildings. The anonymous factor can also be quite fascinating. Working for a university, I have had the honour to sit in the living rooms of intellectual, cultural and community celebrities. I have seen private art collections that reduced me to tears. I have held books signed by Mark Twain. I have touched the relics of Saints. This has been less of a career and more of an adventure. Like Indiana Jones, I search the earth for great cultural treasures and secure them for public engagement and education.

The innovation of donors when freed from the constraints of campaigns and Cases for Support has been exhilarating and inspirational. I truly respect the work of my peers who grind through events to keep the lights on, but I've seen how letting donors *dream* can create powerful results. When working with people connected to a cause, you realize that they know what has stood in the way of progress for a generation. You see that they have worked hard for their money and you understand that it's time for them to speak up! When these donors make a philanthropic plan, they are putting their money where their values are. More and more I am helping to create the legacies of charity executives, staff and people who are connected to the cause but have felt powerless to affect the administration of an organization.

The biggest challenge for the growth of this work in fundraising is that planned giving-trained fundraisers are seen as tax-sorcerers and philanthro-alchemists. I have been told forever by peers, *"Oh, I could never do that."*

I will confess dear reader that I, Paul Nazareth, studied English literature and history. I'm a published poet and classically trained violinist. I do not like math, calculus or algebra. And yet I've spent the past 13 years learning the small calculations and strategies of this type of fundraising because of the multiplication effect it has on the good intentions of donors. Things like:

• *Turning collections of stamps and coins into donations to do good.*

• *Helping seniors on a fixed income donate stocks and securities to save more on tax and keep more cash in their pocket, helping them to give more by giving less!*

• *Explaining to advisors that they can empower clients through tax planned philanthropy by turning a bequest of a few hundred thousand into more than a million dollars using life insurance.*

Why do the donors and I brave the numbers? To change the world for others in ways that did not exist for their generation when they were growing up: education for women; opportunities for immigrants and entrepreneurs; food for the hungry; homes for the homeless; compassion for the mentally-ill and maybe even save this planet we're surfing through space on at the same time.

Now, it's not all fun and games. Charities need to stay close to their strengths and capabilities. Like so many fundraisers I almost burnt out of the profession (and life) because I was trying to do everything at once instead of asking "what makes us revenue?" For-profit companies live by this code, fundraisers for "social-profit" need to as well.

My top three suggestions to get more current and deferred gifts:

1. Cover your bases: Stop trying to be in all places at once! We need to engage our staff at all levels in this task as well. Fundraiser-phobia is growing as the myth of overpaid development staff grows and we end up doing more with less. Make sure your website amplifies your personal ability to serve and inform donors about why to give, how to give and what exactly they need to do to get the gift (be it stocks, life insurance, or property) into your hands.

Search engine optimization in the age of Google is very real. Get your profile on CanadaHelps.org, CharityFocus.ca. Social media is where your donors will turn to engage and ask questions. Now you can answer them in real-time! I have a peer who uses social media for no other purpose than to thank donors for all they do.

2. Integrate your ask: Make sure gift planning training is included in every stream of fundraising and keep your language and material simple. Dedicated brochures are not necessary. Including a check box on all outgoing fundraising forms will suffice. Long tax-focused illustrations are also not required, just provide a one-page document online for donors to print and give to their accountant or lawyer.

3. Use professional advisors: Having expert fundraising consultants and professional advisors in law, accounting, financial planning and insurance on speed dial is critical. It's why the *Canadian Association of Gift Planners* identifies advisors as "partners," full members of the association and not external players.

In today's market, the transactions are faster, the clients / donors more impatient. Making sure that the advisors who make big donations happen know who you are, what you can do and where to find you right away is critical. We only have two big bequest resources in the whole country: *The Canadian Book of Charities* and *The Canadian Donors Guide*. Between them, they sit in over 100,000 offices and reach countless more on the web. It costs less to be in them than the paper used in one fundraising mailer.

Every one of these tips have an embarrassing donor interaction behind it. They were learned the hard way over decades of work by myself and my mentors.

The world's demographics are shifting to an older dominated society. In 2013, a baby girl born in Tokyo will have a 1 in 2 chance of living to over 100 years of age and there are currently more adult diapers sold in Japan than diapers for babies. 70 is the new 50 and as baby-boomers age the *"me"* generation is personalizing philanthropy too.

Moving the focus from individual charities to the causes favoured by the individual will be a more professional but more challenging climate for fundraising. The "philosopher's stone," that element to turn goodwill into dollars, will be even more valuable. But don't count out those millennial donors! Come 2015 they will have more buying power than the baby-boomers and will retain that power for the next 40 years. They don't have as much capital but using the web, crowdfunding and social sharing will see them revolutionize how we raise money in 2020. But that is discussion for another book.

I hope this little journey we've taken together has led you to conclude that the secret to planned giving is to focus on the *goodwill* and not the tax-schemes created to take advantage of it. People give because of their heart, not their head.

Planned giving, gift planning, leaving a legacy… It's not sorcery, it's just another fundraising facet of philanthropy.

STEP

9

COMMUNICATIONS PLAN

"...think rather than spend your way into the market!"

A word from George...

Sometimes you need to whisper and sometimes you need to shout. Ask yourself this question — "How do you get your voice heard over all the rest of the charities vying for your donor's mindshare?"

When I first started out in fundraising, having a communications plan wasn't as important as it is today. I would never dispute the point that "people give to people." But, people will also give to organizations they've heard of. Canada's nonprofit sector is already crowded and growing every day. For this reason, building awareness of your mission, your impact and your various campaigns is critical.

So where does the vigilant fundraiser start?
Back at Step 1 of course! What is the Case for Support? What are you asking for?

"Wait!" you say. "We already have a plan. We have a website, a newsletter and various channels that we use to communicate with our donors."

Ok. In that case, I still want you to revisit your case (the most important document you will ever write!) and then you may want to consider a communications audit.

Most organizations will have some form of communications activity taking place. It's hard to function without communications to your various stakeholders.

A communications audit is a strategic tool that takes a snapshot of your current communications efforts and recommends ways to improve so that you can achieve your objectives. (Remember the mantra of a vigilant fundraiser is "continuous improvement." You should always be looking for ways to improve upon existing processes.)

An audit establishes the baseline for what's working and what isn't in your current communication efforts. In the audit you will look at how you're communicating internally; with employees, members of your board of directors, other volunteers and externally — with donors, suppliers / vendors, community partner organizations, the general public and the media.

Consider the issues and image perceptions you are facing as an organization and the communication needs of your target audiences — again, internally and externally. As part of the information gathering process, you should conduct a SWOT analysis — strengths, weaknesses, opportunities, threats — of your organization. This kind of environmental scan will provide valuable information on the current internal and external climate in which your organization operates.

Generally in this part of the review, you will want to talk to people inside and outside the organization about your current communication practices.

For example, **on the internal communications side:**
- *How do people receive information about what is happening in the organization?*
- *What is communicated?*
- *Do people have the opportunity to provide feedback or ask questions about the information they receive?*
- *Is feedback encouraged?*
- *How frequently do people get information?*

On the external side:
- *Do people know what the organization's goals and objectives are as well as current challenges being faced?*
- *How is this information communicated?*
- *How often and using what methods?*
- *Do people have a chance to provide input and feedback to the organization on information they receive?*

The audit also should include any previous and current communications research that the organization may have done and any other relevant reports on the organization's strategic planning or board effectiveness. These documents can provide valuable information about organizational communications that will form the basis of a more focused inquiry that could be conducted.

As you consider an audit, you will want to ask yourself: "What should this review accomplish for my organization? What will success look like at the end of this process and how will we measure it?" At the conclusion of the audit, you will be well-positioned to effectively navigate Step 9 of the fundraising process.

In the next chapter, **Peter Barrow** argues convincingly for implementation of a structured communications plan. This is documented, measureable activity that will help you to further your goals and remain vigilant in all your stewardship activities. As Peter will show you, a communications plan doesn't have to come with an expensive price tag. Being vigilant also means making the most of your resources at hand.

COMMUNICATIONS:
WHY YOU NEED A PLAN

BY PETER BARROW

Some wise person once wrote that developing a fund-raising program without an effective communications plan to go with it, is like winking at a member of the opposite sex in the dark.

> *Only you know what you are doing
> and you can't see if it's having any effect.*

In spite of this, countless organizations launch into major capital or project-based campaigns without having planned out, and implemented, a comprehensive communications program that will build their brand, raise their profile, tell their story, connect with donors on an emotional level and explain why they need money and how they will spend it.

This often happens because organizations come to the fundraising table with a set of paradigms or boundaries that prevent them from seeing how vital a communications plan is for their survival and success. In summary, these are:

1. *We know all about our organization,*
   so others must know too.

2. *We are passionate about what we do,*
   so everyone must be passionate about it.

3. *We don't need to adapt our current*
   communications efforts — they are doing the job.

4. *We can't afford to spend much money on*
   communications.

5. *We don't have time to do a whole bunch*
   of communicating — we need money NOW!

In almost every case, the reality is very different:

1. *Only those who are completely connected to your*
   organization MAY know all about it. This
   group will not include the hundreds of donors
   who NEED to know.

2. *Your passion will never be felt by others if you*
   don't tell them what to be passionate about.
   The Hospital for Sick Children never assumes that
   everyone is concerned about child mortality; the

United Way never assumes that you understand its community-based philanthropy model.

3. *Most communication programs talk about programs and services, volunteers and day-to-day activities. They DON'T talk about why funds are so vital, what successful outcomes will result if funds are raised, the long-term benefits of a successful campaign – and so on. You need a new story for each new campaign.*

4. *The best communication programs don't need to cost much money. They require creativity, a clear understanding of target markets and an ability to leverage many things you are probably already doing, to achieve success.*

5. *In fundraising, as in life, the best success is achieved by those who plan and execute carefully over time. Jumping in with both feet before you have "informed the market" of your need for money, almost never works.*

DEVELOPING THE PLAN

The best communication plans are:
•*driven by a clear understanding of your target market: who are you trying to reach and why;*
•*reasonably simple, built on four or five things that you do really well and consistently over time;*
•*based on the principle that you should get as much*

*as you can for free — or for a tax receipt, and leverage
everyone you know and every resource you now have;*
- *short-term: you need to come out of the gate fast and be
done in four to six months before the campaign begins;*
- *as creative and unique as possible; and,*
- *Short. Some of the very best plans are only two-three
pages long so everyone can understand and use them.*

KEY COMPONENTS

At minimum, your plan should include:

1. Goals or Objectives: These should be as precise and
measurable as possible, ideally following the SMART
formula (Specific, Measurable, Achievable, Realistic,
and Timely). A goal that says "we will increase awareness of our brand" is fine but hard to measure. A goal
that says "we will increase our brand awareness among
the top 100 business people in our community" is
much better.

2. Target markets: A clear list of who you want to
reach (usually groups, not individuals).

3. Key messages: Short, memorable, emotionally
appealing and easy to remember, the key messages will
underpin everything you do and run "like a golden
thread" through all of your communication pieces.

This is one area where a professional firm may be able
to help *(but, pro bono is the goal — see below!)*. Great

messaging that truly reflects who you are, what you do and why you matter to the donor group is often tough to achieve. Remember that a great message implies benefits to the donor group rather than features about you.

"Cancer can be beaten."
— *Canadian Cancer Society*
"Everyone knows someone who is helped by
the United Way."
— *United Way Canada*
"Discoveries lead to recoveries."
— *The Hospital for Sick Children*
"Every child deserves a bright future."
— *The Children's Foundation of Guelph and Wellington*

These are all examples of messages that develop both emotional appeal and giving impact.

4. Strategies / Tactics / Methods: Classic marketing suggests that strategies and tactics should be two different things.

•*Strategies* are the big picture overview of what you need to do. For example, if a goal is to build brand awareness among 100 more top business people in your community over the next six months, a strategy might be to "Develop three key relationship-building events to which the business community is invited."

•*Tactics* are usually how you achieve the strategies and thus goals. It encompasses the actual "hands on," day-to-day trench work that gets the job done. Ideally, (as noted) only three to five tactics at most, so that you can control and manage them and use your resources prudently. These might include:

- ✔ Two traditional *media-based* initiatives. For example, a newsletter *(or e-newsletter)* along with limited media advertising or a media relations program. (See Step 10 on planned giving newsletters.)

- ✔ One *social media* strategy *(perhaps using Twitter or LinkedIn to build highly targeted awareness, or a Facebook page to build a giving community).* Just remember that all social media strategies take time and skill to manage, so make sure you have both available to you, before launching in.

- ✔ One *relationship-building* strategy: open houses, information sessions, lunches with key donors; speaking engagements, etc. To stay consistent with the earlier example – a sample tactic would be to "host two open houses, specifically for business people and with a business focus."

- ✔ One *traditional print* piece *(separate from the campaign literature)* that clearly spells out who you are, what you do and why / how you do it. This can be used for general mailing and distribution, speaking engagements, conferences, donor meetings and many other purposes.

Obviously, you need to be sensible about this. If you clearly need more strategies to cast a wider net amongst potential donors, then go for it. But, generally, the concept of "less is more" applies well. Doing a few things very well and consistently is much better than the opposite.

BUDGET AND RESOURCES

This is where your creativity and ingenuity must come into play. Unless you have a very strong marketing / communications department and budget *(which few do)*, you need to leverage existing skills and talents as much as possible to stretch your resources to the fullest. Some ways to do this include:

✔ Developing an inventory of related skills from your existing volunteer base: do you have writers, photographers, speakers, graphic artists, and/or printers that you can ask for "that extra mile" of help or to donate services?

✔ If you have high schools in your area, can the marketing / communication or graphic arts classes help you as part of their volunteer service commitment?

✔ Local universities or community colleges also

offer marketing classes that can take on projects as part of their work experience or course requirements. This is especially true when it comes to logo design or other graphics requirements.

✔ Take full advantage of technology and existing sites to source what you need. There are a variety of service providers who can give you outstanding logo design at very economical prices.

✔ Many local media will have special rates for charitable advertising or may donate ad space in return for campaign sponsorship. This is also true of marketing companies, which donate service or expertise and benefit from being listed as a Gold or Platinum campaign sponsor, giving "gifts in kind."

✔ Your volunteer base also will have many other contacts and connections that may be helpful. Again, gather an inventory and then work out how best to use the names you collect.

The key here is to *think* rather than *spend* your way into the market. Almost all of the very best communication campaigns are successful because they were creative, not expensive.

THE FINAL KEY COMPONENT

5. Actions and timelines: Finally, you need to spell out clearly who will undertake the various tactics and when initiatives should be launched and run. A simple critical path can be developed on an Excel spreadsheet that lists the tactics on the left, the timeline in months across the top and a demarcation (x) to show when each will run and for how long.

If you are able to follow this step-by-step process, you will have a strong, workable, easily understood communications plan that helps you to build your brand, connect to the audience, tell your story and, most important of all, raise money!

STEP

10

MARKETING THROUGH A NEWSLETTER

———

"When organizations decide not to build a house subscriber list and send out newsletters on a regular basis, they are missing out on an important opportunity..."

A word from George...

For me Step 10 is pretty straight forward. You <u>need</u> to develop and maintain a regular newsletter. The type of newsletter will depend on your communications plan and the audience that you're talking to. I've seen them used in a variety of ways: one organization that I've worked with does a quarterly newsletter that is tied into their annual giving campaign. It is a passive ask, mailed with an envelope, but it works as part of their fundraising strategy.

I know of another example where an organization was considering changing their newsletter into an electronic format. Feedback from the donors that this charity worked with indicated that they wanted the newsletter to remain a hard-copy printed hand-out. This was a nonprofit that dealt with bereaved families. It turned out that many of the families involved in the charity had an emotional connection to content that was in the newsletter. They wanted to keep it nearby so they could re-read it when the need moved them. The newsletter clearly bonded stakeholders and the organization together in the work that was being done.

All too often organizations say they don't publish a newsletter because it is too hard or too expensive to generate the content required to make each issue interesting. "We just don't have the resources or the budget." In my experience, a vigilant fundraiser can't *afford to overlook this important communications tool.*

*As **Ed Sluga** explains, a newsletter will be most <u>effective</u> when integrated with other elements of your marketing mix. He also introduces the idea of targeting your newsletter to a planned giving audience. A newsletter may be your way of improving on Step 8. Think about it.*

MARKETING THROUGH A NEWSLETTER: IT'S ABOUT DONOR ENGAGEMENT

BY ED SLUGA

For many charities, creating a newsletter is their first step to promoting their organization and is used as a means to engage their best and most loyal donors in their fund development program. In recent years, and with the advent of digital technologies, this type of engagement has become viewed as "old fashioned" and too expensive. Why not just drive users to the organizational website? Or, get them to follow tweeted updates on Twitter? Or, become friends on Facebook? But the fact is that these new media – although exciting and filled with low-cost potential do not work for most not-for-profits when used in isolation.

A newsletter remains the cornerstone to an integrated "brand publishing" approach. What a not-for-profit wishes to accomplish through its marketing – and needs to achieve at as low a cost as possible – is *engagement* of their stakeholders with what the organization does.

Too often organizations try to "sell' to their constituents.

But the notion of "selling" is outdated – even in the business world. Connecting with people's values and beliefs is the key to what successful marketing manages to achieve.

What this means is that organizations must think beyond their outward "marketing" to individuals and instead, develop a program for full engagement between the individual and the mission of the organization. But often, the mission and principles and beliefs of the organization are as complex as those beliefs that we individuals abide by. They are hard to explain and difficult to remember. As a result, it becomes the responsibility of the organization to reinforce these core values at every opportunity so that all donors and supporters are made aware of the fundamental positions of the organization and feel as though they are invited to be a full partner in the organization's mission.

Try accomplishing that in 140 characters or through posts on a blog!

But this is not to say that the social media channels of marketing aren't important. New technologies must work in association with more established forms of marketing – fully developed newsletters for example – to create an integrated approach to donor engagement.

In the varied levels of the case statement matrix, the vast majority of charities do not have emergent need. In fact, well-run and developed charities wish to avoid emergent need. As a result, the immediacy of social media channels is a function that remains largely under-developed. It is also why the use of newsletters to engage the core audience of a nonprofit organization remains the current best practice for charities.

Newsletters remain the flagship information piece for a long-term, established development program for many reasons, but their greatest advantage is *the form* in which they present information to the charity's donors. It is a type of engagement that older donors in particular — which typically remain the charitable sector's best donors — understand and have become accustomed to for much of their lives.

Of course, newsletters cannot continue to work in isolation or removed from newer alternative forms of digital marketing activity. They have become part of an integrated system that links and re-links back to other varied forms of communication. In essence, newsletters remain a channel of communication that is imperative to have, but only when integrated with all the other various forms of marketing that are currently available to the nonprofit sector.

THE MARKETING MIX

To understand why newsletters are so vital to donor engagement, it is important to understand marketing as it relates to the donation cycle.

When people or organizations are involved on a

voluntary basis – each contributing something of value to an exchange and communicating with each other about it – a relationship exists. This relationship can be short-term and/or transient, or it can be long-term, existing over a number of years.

The concept of "relationship" is seminal to success for a charity. As such, developing, maintaining and strengthening relationships is crucial to the success of all strategic fundraising programs. Newsletter marketing – when integrated with all the other forms of marketing – is a tool used to "publish" the mission and Case for Support and successfully communicate the principles and beliefs of a charity that sees relationship-building as the key to successful fundraising.

The entire package of co-ordinated activities is the marketing program, the elements of which are known as the *"marketing mix."* The components of the marketing mix are those factors controlled by, and/or varied by the marketer in an attempt to fulfill the objectives of the marketing plan.

If the marketing situation warrants it, the marketing mix can become quite complex and sophisticated. In these cases, a great deal of detailed market research is commonplace as is the further break-down of the four marketing elements (product, pricing, placement and promotion or, as is suggested in Step 11, the five 'c's) into a large number of sub-elements – each requiring close scrutiny and interpretation. This is predominantly seen in business where there is considerable margin to absorb the overhead costs of this kind of high-level marketing. It is most often associated with packaged goods or certain products such as automobiles.

IT'S STILL
ABOUT YOUR MISSION

Charities must aim to fulfill two separate and distinct functions when marketing to its different groups: client / users and potential donors. The challenge here is clear. You are talking to two audiences with vastly differing focuses. Yet, the challenge can be met and goals achieved, when your organization utilizes the entire set of marketing mix elements at its disposal.

Not-for-profit organizations market to a diverse group of contributor types that include volunteers, annual donors, major gift donors, and potential planned giving donors. Potential planned giving donors, who have by definition, made a long-term commitment to the charitable organization, require an appropriate mix of marketing elements to secure their continued financial support. Yet, like the two faces of Janus, the two marketing programs (one directed to client / users, and one directed to potential contributors) are not independent of each other. Successful gift planning marketers understand the significance of one overriding factor – the effect that one program will have on the other.

Thus, it is clear that the marketing program is not "selling" donation products. Rather, the marketing program is primarily concerned with promoting the mission and objectives of the charity and continually highlighting its brand. In marketing to potential donors and encouraging them to invest in the charity, the organization must position its message beyond "product" (programs and services) to appeal to the donor's core values.

The second function of marketing is the promotion of the actual instruments of support. These "products" – in the business sense – are used as the way the individual supports the mission and vision of the charity. They are best marketed as a means and structure of support.

When one realizes that the activities of "brand publishing" must be approached much like successful brands in the business world, it becomes obvious that the vigilant organization must create a cornerstone and tangible vehicle to lead this endeavour. This initiative will be the starting point of a relationship-building dialogue that must end with the donor feeling like a partner in the mission of the organization. A newsletter is the tool you need. When working in association with the other elements of the marketing program it becomes the best way to fulfill your marketing objectives.

STEP

11

MAKING THE CASE
FOR CREATIVE

---

*"Sometimes campaign volunteers use
the marketing material as a shield."*

A word from George...

At some point, likely around Step 5 or Step 6, you will have realized a hard truth. Many volunteers are afraid of fundraising. They are afraid to make themselves vulnerable, <u>afraid</u> to be embarrassed and afraid of embarrassing the prospective donor they are meeting with.

As already discussed, there are a few fundamental things that you can do to take away some of your volunteer's fear. Proper recruitment and expectation setting is important. Training is vital. A third, and often overlooked aspect of the training piece is the promotional material that you provide to your fundraising volunteers and staff. The communication material that you produce will:

- give a volunteer confidence by providing words that reinforce the message they are delivering

- reassure both volunteer and donor that your charity is professional in its conduct and how it approaches its fundraising activity

- allow your fundraisers to demonstrate their preparation for the fundraising call

- provide a leave-behind that generates the possibility of a future conversation and further engagement with the charity

Determining the needs of your charity when it comes to the creation of promotional material can be a challenge. Enter **John VanDuzer**. As a long-time creative director in the not-for-profit sector, he has witnessed a lot of changes to the approach that charities need to take to stay alive in an increasingly competitive market.

In Step 11 he demonstrates that a vigilant fundraiser not only needs to utilize promotional material, they need to understand the market that they're working in.

It's better to ride the wave...

than to get caught under it.

THE 'C' CHANGE:
MAKING THE CASE FOR CREATIVE

BY JOHN VANDUZER

Like waves in the ocean, it's relentless and it's constant. Change is ever-flowing. Change is ever-changing. For years, communication professionals have been trying to catch the wave only to be overwhelmed by a surge of water seeking to drown them. Destroy them. Pound them into the surf and sand.

Overly dramatic? Maybe yes. Maybe no.

Think back to the days of yore, to the days when Madison Avenue (or Toronto's Bloor Street) really did rule. Advertising told us what to believe and we did. We were sold. But those days are gone and marketing has struggled to regain its footing ever since.

Of course, in the nonprofit sector we've never had the upper hand in terms of our communications. Where consumer brands have traditionally looked down on their consumers, we've always been the opposite, looking up from bended knee, asking (or begging) for a few dollars more. But even in the charitable sector things have been changing at an increasingly rapid rate.

The challenges that you're experiencing aren't unique to you or your organization. Waves of rapid change are breaking on our shores every hour of every day. In this chapter we explore the subject of creativity in the context of the 12-Step Fundraising program, and offer a creative approach to sea change or, as we call it, a "C" change.

First things first: what's a "C" change? Drawn from the phrase in the song, *"Full Fathom Five"* in Shakespeare's *"The Tempest,"* a sea change is generally regarded as a profound change or transformation. A different way to look at "C" change is to be able to "see" change.

Literally.

To see change is to be aware of how the world is changing or needs to change.

We will explore both types of "seeing" as we consider best practices in terms of developing creative in the current nonprofit sector.

WHAT IS MEANT BY THE "C" CHANGE

Is your consumer a cat or a dog? No, really. If our communications are any indication, the answer is clear: they're dogs — faithful, loyal, eager to please. Only they aren't. They're cats. Let me explain.

The way we market – the way we draft a fundraising appeal – assumes that prospects will listen and respond accordingly. We expect they will "obey" the logic of our argument, story or case and that they will "bite."

We believe donors love us as we are and will respond favourably.

Pardon the pun, but donors aren't dogs, they're cats.

They like you well enough, but they love themselves more. They'll ignore what you have to say, "hiss" if it appears you've spent too much money, or turn, flick their tail and walk away if you don't hook them in the opening paragraph of your annual fund letter.

Dogs, for the most part, come when you call them. They are known as man's best friend. Dogs will fetch on command and they love you as you are. You exist to serve them. Dogs exist to serve you. So doggone it, generating a response from a group of prospective consumers, clients and customers is a lot like herding cats.

Our thesis is that as marketers, as marketing people, as communications professionals we're still treating our consumers, our clients, our constituents as if they're dogs and then act surprised when something doesn't work.

AND THERE'S THE CLIMATE CHANGE

No, not global warming but, rather, the "chill" charities are getting. With more and more charities sending out more and more letters and tweets and making more and more calls, we live in an environment that's less charitable, more combative and certainly more competitive.

Mess up once and you're through. There's no second chance; there's no second opportunity to make a first impression. This even applies to clients and members with whom you've had an ongoing relationship. All of a sudden you're just not pals anymore. This combativeness and conflict shows itself in consumer antipathy – "I don't believe you." Or maybe it's just apathy. Donor fatigue it's called.

A CINDERELLA COMPLEX

Cinderella from folklore and Disney is your client. Your offer needs to fit and fit perfectly. "On demand" print-ing and social media provide charities with unprec-edented opportunities to target prospects one at a time. A direct mail appeal with twelve variables is great if it's going out to twelve people. But for 1,000 prospects do whatever you can to target them individually and you'll get a much better response. And live happily ever after.

Cinderella's shoe only fit Cinderella. Why? Because it was made for her and only her. The charitable fairies and magical mice didn't go to Payless or search one of the stepsister's closets; it was made to measure.

Donors don't want what you have to offer. They want what they want. They want your proposal, your opportunity, your ask to "fit" them as perfectly as the glass slipper fit Cinderella's tiny foot.

When the shoe doesn't fit, you try to push the foot in. It only hurts and hurts the relationship.

The shoe has to fit!

CAPTURING THE CLICK GENERATION

The "net generation," or those born after 1980 or 1985, is all about multi-tasking. Distraction is their attraction; it's all they've ever known. When marketing to the net generation think of them as the "click" generation – clicking between screens, between apps, between experiences in seconds.

Grab their attention fast. Expect to keep it for a few seconds or minutes at most. Get in and out fast. Or, with a click of their mouse or thumb on their smart phone you'll be gone; out in the ether.

But click is more than just the click of a mouse. Does your message click with your consumer? You can be *"waa, waa, waa Charlie Brown"* – remember Charlie Brown and the teachers? You never saw the adults and you never heard the adults except to say *"waa, waa, waa."* Now we're back to cats and dogs again. What do they hear? It's *"waa, waa, waa, Fluffy"* and it's *"waa, waa, waa, food."* All they hear is what they want to hear and everything else is just noise. So you have to make sure that your message clicks – resonates – with consumers and again it's on their terms, not yours. And it's got to be done fast.

Choose the right words and you will carry the right meaning. Choose the wrong words, and the meaning is out the door. And please, please, please do not try to please everyone. If you try to please everyone, you will please absolutely no one. And finally, don't over stuff the message.

Keep it short.
Keep it simple.
Click with your target or "click" you'll be gone.

CONTROL: GET OVER IT

Mario Andretti once said, "If you're in control, you're not going fast enough." Given the speeds at which these guys (and gals) are driving that's a little insane but he makes a good point. It used to be that you could control your message. No more. Not with social media especially. Get used to it. Because the biggest risk you can make is not to take risks. Play it safe and you'll finish last. No risk? No reward. So the issue of control is one that a lot of people wrestle with.

CRISIS? WHAT CRISIS?!

With apologies to the seventies' supergroup Super-tramp (this was the title of one of their early albums), the dire consequences of most of our appeals are crises *we've* created, not our donors. And so they should be excused for not believing the sky is falling just because we tell them so. Like the boy who cried "wolf," we can't continue to operate in a state of crisis with every communication we send. Bad news stories need to appear alongside good news stories. Show the impact of what their gifts have accomplished instead of running around yelling *"fire!"* every five minutes.

MOVING ON: THE 5 P's BECAME THE 5 C's

Marketing 101 brought with it five P's of positioning: product, price, place, packaging and promotion. Take water. You can only really buy two kinds: sparkling and flat. While, yes, there are obvious differences between water with bubbles and water without, all things being equal, water is water and the difference, if any, between one brand and another is slight. Yes, the *product* is essentially the same.

The *price* for Evian, Perrier, Dasani and the like are all pretty much the same (which is to say "a lot" when you consider that tap water is free) and they're all available wherever beverages are sold (*place*).

Packaging has come a long way in recent years with

ever more clever containers tantalizing our eyes before our lips ever touch the spout, but for the most part competing water brands are sold in equivalent sizes and in plastic translucent or transparent bottles. The only real defining element between bottled water brands (and we could argue beers, wines, colas and even to some degree, cars) is *promotion*.

The battle of the commodity brands has, for years, been fought on one relatively crowded battlefield; on one of the five 'P' platforms: promotion.

But you say, *"John, we're not in the packaged goods industry. We're a nonprofit; a charity. There's a difference."* Well, yes. And no. Sure, there's a huge difference between consumables and charities but, truthfully, the opposite remains true, too. In Canada there are some 80,000 registered charities competing for attention in only a very few categories:

1. Arts & Culture
2. Community / Social Service
3. Education
4. Healthcare
5. Religious
6. International

All are trying to do "good" and most are worthy of people's donations. But differentiating between one donor appeal and another often comes down to one thing: promotion. Or, in the new and ever-changing world: creative.

Because just as the seas change, so too have we seen that the traditional 5 P's have been replaced by the 5 C's:

THAT WAS THEN... The Five P's of Positioning	THIS IS NOW... The Five C's of Creative
Product	Consumer
Price	Clear
Packaging	Credible
Place	Competitive
Promotion	Consistent

Knowing that the change has taken place and knowing what to make of this change will mean the difference to ensuring that your charity survives and thrives in the years to come.

1. CONSUMER

More than ever before, everything starts and ends with the consumer. If you're not consumer-focused you're dead (or soon will be). Much has been made about the importance of donors but as a sector, our creative leaves a lot to be desired. It costs a lot of money for not enough return on investment.

So what are charities doing?
Hiring cheaper help and getting even worse results.

"Donors don't give *to* your organization, they give *through* your organization to fix a problem they worry about; sustain or expand a solution they believe in; get more of what they're interested in; or in order to feel like they've made a difference," says Tom Ahern, a self-described "persuasion engineer" who writes, trains and consults.

Following through on his logic, what he's saying is that when people make a donation to, say, the Memphis Child Advocacy Centre, they are not giving to that centre but *through* that centre because they believe in the centre's mission which is "Helping victims become children again."

He's right.

Donors don't give to you they give through you. It's, therefore, incumbent on charities to communicate clearly and concisely and use compelling examples. Present who you are, what you do and how people's donation will make a difference. As attractive as the vehicle is, people only buy cars, vans or trucks to get from where they are to where they want to go.

Your charity is a vehicle, not a destination.

People don't trust you because they understand you; they trust you because they feel themselves to be understood. And if the understanding is mutual the relationship will be rewarded.

We struggled with the brightest marketing minds at Sunnybrook Health Sciences to come up with a slogan that would help to not just brand a capital fundraising campaign but the Hospital, too. After more than twenty serious submissions we finally hit the jackpot and in the context of this example it should come as no surprise that it was one that focused on the consumer: *When it matters most.*

If you're in a terrible accident you hope to be airlifted to Sunnybrook where their Emergency and Trauma Unit is the best in the country. If you've been diagnosed with breast cancer it matters to you and your family that you be treated at Sunnybrook. And for the brave men and women who fought when it mattered most to Canada's safety as a nation, it matters that veterans receive specialized care at Sunnybrook. "When it matters most" was focused on the people Sunnybrook serves.

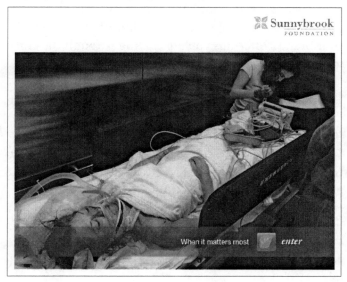

Creative: wishart.net

> *Harley Davidson doesn't sell motorcycles;*
> *it sells 43-year-old accountants the opportunity*
> *to dress up in black leather, drive through*
> *small towns and have people be afraid of them.*
> — *Tom Peters*

2. LET'S BE CLEAR

To be clear is to speak with clarity. Branding aims to establish a significant and differentiated place in the market in order to attract and retain consumers.

A strong brand is nothing more than a firm and authentic foundation upon which a bond can be built between your charity's vision and a community of like-minded people. When people see something of themselves in your brand's offerings you are cutting through the clutter of millions of marketing messages.

To do this you must be clear. Muddled messages never make it. Be clear. And to be clear you must be concise. "Cancer can be beaten," the Canadian Cancer Society once said. And for a time this message was clear. But times changed. More clarity was needed. And so for a planned giving campaign for Toronto's Princess Margaret Hospital — one of if not *the* leading cancer hospitals in the country — wishart created the phrase "Conquer Cancer." Why beat cancer when you can conquer it?! Stronger, clearer communications are — and always will be — needed.

3. BE INCREDIBLY CREDIBLE

The box in the lower corner covers up the logo. So name the brand that this double page spread is advertising. No, it's not hardwood floors although guessing that makes sense. The homeowner would much rather take off her heels and walk barefoot on her floors. We get it but, no, you're wrong. You'd also be wrong if you guessed shoes *(lame)*, or even Viagra *(get your mind out of the gutter)*!

Creative: Ogilvy & Mather, Canada for Mattel Inc.

Give up? It's an ad for Hot Wheels. Yes, Hot Wheels! And we love it because it's so unexpected, so real and, yes, so credible. You've got to know that whoever created and approved this ad has kids. But not just young kids: boys. This is what boys do, they see shoes and think "I'm gonna jump my Hot Wheels up and over one and land them on the other." This is 20, 30 or 40 minutes of fun. Time spent away from the computer, or TV.

In a magazine saturated with inflated claims about every conceivable product comes this oasis of calm. It's an ad that demands a lot of its reader and hits the proverbial ball out of the park.

When SickKids launched a $100 million campaign it did so with the simplest and most credible of slogans: *"Help make Sick Kids Better."* And donors did. Because they believed they could make a difference. And so they did!

4. THE COMPETITION BUREAU

We need to be competitive. Competitive is not just saying, "I'm better than you." Back to the consumer again: It's about being competitive in the mind of the consumer.

When you think Kleenex, you think tissue. You don't say, "Can I have a tissue?" You say, "I need Kleenex." Now if someone gives you a Scotties tissue you're going to take it, especially if your nose is dripping. But the point is that Kleenex "owns" tissue. No other brand comes close.

When you think Volvo, even if you're not a car aficionado, you know Volvo stands for "safety." In Europe they've described the car as a cage that saves lives. That's what you're buying; you're buying safety.

> *Band-Aid is adhesive bandages.*
> *Nobody says, "Can I have an adhesive bandage?"*
> *That would just be weird.*

And if you're thinking of buying a dependable washer or dryer you can't help but think of Maytag and the Maytag repairman. That guy is still bored after all these years. He's so bored that he died and they've gone through two other Maytag guys in the interim who are still just as equally bored and who will probably die at some point and be replaced.

The point is, that just as you think you're getting bored with your brand imagery people are just getting used to it and some are finally seeing it for the very first time — which leads to the fifth and final "C."

5. CONSISTENTLY CONSISTENT

Consistent means over time, not overnight. Truly, what you do today may not impact tomorrow but if it's consumer-centred, clear, credible and competitive and if it's applied consistently then your tomorrows will be brighter, I promise you.

Here's proof:

- Quick, name a mouse that makes kids squeal with delight?
- Name a soup that's *"mmm, mmm good?"*
- What's got *"two all beef patties, special sauce, lettuce, cheese on a sesame seed bun?"*
- Thirsty? It's *"the real thing."*
- A battery that *"keeps going, and going, and going..."*

Our experience is that people give up on their brand at precisely the moment that their prospects are just catching on to them. Don't give up too soon.

Creative: wishart.net

Although it's been over 10 years since the last telethon t-shirt was printed, teddy bears remain synonymous with SickKids. For more than a decade, wishart created beautiful, collectable *"Wear Your Bear"* merchandise. Not only did this help the SickKids' telethon raise millions of dollars each year, but sales of these wearable ads raised millions more. One great idea re-imagined year-after-year-after-year: it's how the best stand out.

IN CONCLUSION

More is less, more or less. With costs to get your message out plummeting, it's all too easy to get carried away and send out an email to 2 million prospects instead of 2,000 donors.

Don't overload the boat or it will sink. Instead, think of your creative as a one-to-one relationship between you in the stern and your donor in the bow of your canoe. Every stroke you take affects the journey you take with that donor and the opposite is true, too. But we're Canadians and canoes are the way to go.

If you're not centred on the customer, and if your communications aren't clear, credible, competitive and done consistently over time then your time will soon be up!

Creative can bring your case, your appeal, your message to life but it must abide by the 5 C's lest you get drowned by the waves of unrelenting change.

BEING VIGILANT

"The truly vigilant fundraiser is one that is constantly on the lookout for opportunities to support an organization's long-term sustainability..."

A word from George...

This is it. You've reached the final step in the fundraising process.

*But here's the kicker. You can have the first 11 steps in place and still have only average results. Why is that? What is that "thing" that sets some charities so far above the rest? You know what I'm going to say — it's <u>vigilance</u> and if we haven't sold you on the concept yet, the final chapter is sure to tip you to the other side. In Step 12, **Jim Watson and I** are going show you why <u>vigilance</u> is the secret ingredient that will make the previous steps — all best practice activities — work for your organization.*

There are two types of fundraisers out there. There are the ones work from their office — often closed off from people and outside interactions. Then there is the fundraiser who is truly "out there," being vigilant to opportunities and meeting the people who make magic happen.

I get frustrated when I see fundraisers eating lunch at their desks instead of going to the cafeteria and interacting with people around them. A fundraiser's network starts where they live. Vigilance starts when you open yourself up to the possibilities of what is happening around you.

Put on your entrepreneurial hat. Success will come when you recognize opportunity and act on it. Steps 1 through 11 gives you the tools and makes you prepared. Step 12 is your call to action.

Get out from behind your desk. Push boundaries. Try something new, but only if it's within your mandate to do so. Steward your donors. Measure success. Create benchmarks. Capitalize on opportunities and invite feedback. This is what it means to be a vigilant fundraiser.

BEING VIGILANT

BY JIM WATSON & GEORGE STANOIS

In November 2012, Toronto and Calgary faced off in the annual Canadian Football League Grey Cup finals. The Ontario and Alberta Premiers made a public wager on the outcome of the game – the loser would donate 100 items of warm clothing to the winner's chosen charity.

The Ontario Premier's team won, and he selected the Red Door Family Shelter in Ontario. The unexpected gift provided the charity with the opportunity to raise its profile – both the Premier and offensive guard Joe Eppele of the Toronto Argonauts delivered the items to the shelter's administrative office, warranting a press release, photographs, and unexpected media coverage.

It was the sort of pleasant surprise that couldn't possibly have been part of the charity's fundraising strategy. In this position, however, many a clever fundraiser could grasp the opportunity to build upon the positive profile. A few phone calls or letters could turn the gesture into a mini-campaign for short-term needs. The theme could be used for a recurring gifts drive. We can see it now: Football for Fleece! Touchdowns for Toques!

If you've followed the first 11 steps of this book, you're the proud owner of a clearly defined case for support and fundraising strategy. You'll have a dedicated group of volunteers following your advice on "making the ask." Your robust communications plan ensures that your target audiences get the message, fulfill the call to action, and feel recognized for their contributions.

One final, vital question remains. Are you being vigilant? Could you take a high-profile gesture and turn it into a windfall? Do you know how to determine when your plan has been a success?

WHAT IS VIGILANCE?

Vigilance is associated — but should not be confused — with meeting a fundraising target. While it does take a certain amount of vigilance to crack that goal of, say, one million dollars, the truly vigilant fundraiser is one that is constantly on the lookout for opportunities to support an organization's long-term sustainability.

We like Jim's advice to clients to "plan your work and work your plan." Vigilance means having a keen sense of when to push boundaries or try something new, but always using your strategy's clear mandate to drive those decisions.

WHAT DOES "SUCCESS" LOOK LIKE?

A successful campaign yields more than just funds – it provides potent information for future use and planning. Step 2 discussed how to develop a sound fundraising strategy.

> *The vigilant fundraiser looks for ways to make the most of this experience, learning from the past to plan for the future.*

How does this work?

Develop metrics for success. Review past campaign strategies and results. Use this information – and, if you like, information from similar organizations – to create benchmarks. This process will help you set reasonable expectations and guide your strategy. Later, comparing your results to your benchmark will help you to assess your performance and better plan future campaigns.

Create a system for feedback. Take the pulse of your team – staff, board, and volunteers – as well as your trusted peers and frequent donors. What kinds of questions will help you gather useful information? How are you doing? Do they have ideas to contribute?

Assess your data. What worked? What didn't work? Did you meet or exceed your goals? Take stock of your plan and performance, and consider all feedback. If you're really gung ho, poll peers in similar organizations. How have they set goals and bench-marked for success?

Consider the whole organization. Complete a 360-degree review of your whole organization. All activities have the potential to affect your strategy. If all departments are aligned and work toward similar goals, you'll have a better chance of success.

EYES OPEN, EAR TO THE GROUND

Survival — and success — depends on doing more with less. Survivors keep their eyes open and their ears to the ground. They may have limited budgets, but they recognize opportunity and find creative ways to pounce.

As we learned in Step 9, creativity doesn't have to be expensive. Make friends with the media and remind them that you can provide "talking heads" on your topic at a moment's notice. Offer your organization's expertise for talks at local business associations, clubs, and forums. Set up promotional partnerships with allied organizations. You can also look to the private sector for ideas and tools. To get the creative juices flowing, here are a few ideas for building your audience and sharing your message.

Make technology work for you. YouTube is free. Same with Twitter, Facebook, and LinkedIn. Which platforms does your targeted audience use? Does a social media campaign make sense for your organization? How can you use it to your advantage? In a notorious campaign against coal, GreenPeace used Facebook's terminology to advocate "unfriending" the resource. Over 500,000 people signed the online anti-Facebook petition and more than 330,000 watched the campaign video, which featured Facebook's CEO, Mark Zuckerberg. With web analytics programs *(also free)* the response is easily tracked.

Try your hand at "guerilla" marketing. Guerilla marketing is a low-cost, unconventional approach to promotion that often takes advantage of a specific place or gathering to reach a targeted audience. Here's one example. Prior to the release of one of the films in the Twilight series, marketers hijacked pictures of models in existing bus shelter ads to make "vampire victims" using branded red dot stickers. Easy, cheap, and effective!

Hold an unprecedented event. In Step 3, we discuss the potential for events to be powerful experiences. They don't have to cost a fortune, either. When properly executed, a free event can provide a similar impact, building your organization's profile and drawing positive attention to your cause. Forget flash mobs — instead, hold a "cash" mob! As part of a statement against pro-life activism, a group of people gathered at Planned Parenthood and raised $2,000 in minutes in October 2012.

With each of these measures, remember that it's important to take the time to know your targeted audience. Explore other areas that interest the people you're trying to reach. If you discover that a large percentage of your supporters are also football fans, a CFL-sponsored gift drive might just work. The vigilant fundraiser is always on the lookout for these types of opportunities.

BE PREPARED

Like the Boy Scouts say, be prepared! It is one thing to be observant but quite another to recognize an opportunity and then effectively act on it. Everything you've learned in Chapters 1-11 will help you to make the most of unexpected circumstances. Setting the stage to collect information will help you evaluate your success year after year, so that you will be better prepared when the Premier comes knocking at your organization's red door.

ABOUT THE AUTHORS

PETER BARROW was Chair of the Children's Foundation of Guelph and Wellington for seven years and is now past Chair. He serves as incoming Vice President of the Board of Directors of Hopewell Children's Homes and is a member of the Campaign Cabinet for the Athletics Department, University of Guelph. The Department is currently raising $30 million as part of the University's Better Planet project.

Peter owns Petrona Associates, a training, facilitation and marketing company and is on the road about 100 days a year with a wide variety of corporate profit clients.

Peter also works with the Goldie Company where he handles marketing and communication strategies for Goldie clients. With Ed Sluga, he co-authored *Worthy and Prepared*, a fundraising how-to book for smaller charities, published by Civil Sector Press in 2009.

Peter and his wife live in Guelph where gardening,

swimming, sports, two sons and two grandchildren take up most of their time. Peter is a graduate of the Carleton University School of Journalism and once ran the Toronto marathon in 2 hours, 48 minutes.

GINA EISLER, MA, CFRE started working in the non-profit field in 1988 after graduating with a Bachelor of Arts degree in English Literature and Sociology from the University of Winnipeg. Gina has worked with health charities since 1992, including two children's hospitals, three long-term care facilities, two teaching / research facilities and four community hospitals.

Gina started working on major gifts campaigns in 1992 at Health Sciences Centre Foundation in Winnipeg. Since then she has directed major gifts campaigns with goals ranging from $1.2 million to $100 million. Her experience includes major gifts, capital campaigns, annual appeals, special events and planned giving.

As an active volunteer with the Association for Healthcare Philanthropy, Gina has been part of the Primer Faculty for seven years, and Canadian Chair of the one-day Introduction to Healthcare Philanthropy Primer since 2006.

In her spare time, she races her sailboat, Scalliwag, on Lake Ontario. Her goal is to participate in ocean races, and with her crew, compete in the Lake Ontario 300, the longest fresh water sailing race in the world.

JENNIFER HILBORN and **SARAH VARLEY** met in 1996 as co-workers in the marketing department for the Swedish Telecom giant Ericsson. Working together they discovered a shared set of fundamental values and forged a powerful connection. When the duo left their global roles at Ericsson in 2001 – Sarah was working with the company's strategy for Entertainment Marketing and Jennifer managed Ericsson's Corporate Social Responsibility program – they formed Esteemed Events.

Sarah and Jennifer's first project was the creation of *The Girl Event*, a self-esteem building event for teenage girls which launched in 2003. The event attracted corporate sponsorship from Hudson Bay Company, Procter & Gamble, Rogers and Universal Music, as well as a nonprofit partnership with YWCA Toronto. In addition, the event received broad media coverage on all major Canadian news networks. Since then, they have built a successful marketing communications agency, working with a varied client list in both nonprofit and for profit sectors. While they share key ideals of integrity, and excellence, Sarah and Jennifer bring very unique gifts to the partnership.

Sarah is a no-nonsense, quick and detailed dynamo whose articulate and self-assured opinions and insights make her an asset in both the creative process and indispensible for on-the-ground activations. Precise logistics and planning are Sarah's modus operandi. She is also a huge advocate for metrics and accountability in sponsorship, so it is fitting that she designed an online tool for Ericsson to evaluate incoming sponsorship requests from around the world. Her 20+ years of volunteer work with Tennis Canada won Sarah the honour of Volunteer of the Year. She also volunteers weekly for Mid Toronto Community Services and their Meals on Wheels program in downtown Toronto where she lives.

Jennifer is the consummate diplomat, hostess and event manager; often seeming most "in-the-zone" when she is in high energy – even high stress situations. From a last minute book-signing tour with Margaret Atwood, while a Key Porter Books publicist, to managing a bevy of disgruntled Ericsson VIP guests trapped at Tremblant in the 1999 ice storm, Jennifer solves problems on her feet and quickly puts her clients at ease. Early on Jennifer emerged as a go-to person for business writing and communications. Her press releases landed many a Canadian author on the coveted CBC Radio program, Morningside with Peter Gzowski. She also authored and launched Ericsson Canada's online newsletter, and created her own column '*bCause*,' for a local Toronto newspaper, ETC News, focusing on socially responsible corporations in her community.

PAUL NAZARETH is a philanthropic advisor with Scotia Private Client Group since 2011. He spent 11 years working in planned giving with charities such as the University of Toronto and Catholic Archdiocese of Toronto. He teaches the national online planned giving course with the Georgian College postgraduate fundraising program and is a national instructor for the Canadian Association of Gift Planners. A former board member of the Canadian Charitable Annuity Association and several charities, Paul is currently chair of the advisory committee of the Humber College Postgraduate Fundraising Program and writes for the publication *"Gift Planning in Canada"* and the Association of Fundraising Professionals.

Paul is a career-long volunteer with CAGP and has won the local Jasmine Sweatman award for volunteer excellence, the ICSC International team award for best planned giving program and speaks about legacy philanthropy across Canada.

LEE PIGEAU has worked as a fundraiser and volunteer in some of Canada's largest cities and smallest rural areas. He is dedicated to community building and helping nonprofit organizations raise funds and manage their operations efficiently and effectively. With 20 years' experience as a fundraiser, leader and volunteer, helping organizations realize their potential is his passion.

Lee started his fundraising career in the social service sector at the United Way of Greater Toronto and went on to the United Way of Edmonton as the senior campaign manager for business and education. In this role, he was a special liaison with several charities serving underprivileged and at-risk youth. Lee was the Campaign Director for Trent University's successful seventeen million dollar "Beyond Our Walls" campaign, Lakehead University's Orillia Campus expansion campaign and was Executive Director of Soldiers' Memorial Hospital Foundation in Orillia. At the present time, he is the Chief Executive Officer at Habitat for Humanity Huronia.

Lee has been a keynote speaker at various Canadian and provincial conferences speaking on strategic planning, volunteer management and motivation, board and staff relations as well fundraising and goal setting.

Lee teaches Volunteer Management, Annual Giving & Planning for Fundraising at Georgian College.

JOHN A. PHIN, CFRE takes great satisfaction in being a professional fundraiser having served a variety of charitable and community-based organizations over the past 30 years. It's this extensive experience that has resulted in the knowledge and skills that make him an accomplished consultant, staff member, teacher, and volunteer.

And it's a fulfilling life. He is currently Director of Resource Development at Hull Services in Calgary, a 50-year-old charity making significant differences in the lives of children and their families. In 2007, he opened Applied Philanthropy Inc. as president to manage his consulting work, and since 2009 has represented The Goldie Company in western Canada. Between 2004 and 2013, he was also busy as a part-time lecturer at Calgary's Mount Royal University teaching Fundraising and Fund Development.

John is a steady advocate for his profession. He earned and maintains the CFRE designation. He is recruited as a speaker on the role of fundraising in charitable organizations. He is an active or past member of several professional associations with local, national and international board and committee experience. For John, fundraising is a mission.

John lives in Calgary with his wife who is the best friend anyone could ever have. They have two sons, amazing young men also dedicated to making the world a better place.

LIZ REJMAN, CFRE has spent her entire career in the not-for-profit sector bringing her dynamic expertise to health care, education and the arts. Her professional focus has been on database management and prospect research for both large and small fundraising shops. She has a particular interest in social media as a research tool, media monitoring, and the effect of the internet filter bubble on balanced research.

For several years, Liz instructed on the topic of prospect research within the Fund Development Program at Georgian College and taught the course Technology in the Not for Profit at Continuing Studies, Western University. Liz has also presented on various topics related to prospect research at conferences for APRA (Association of Professional Researchers in Advancement), AHP (Association of Healthcare Professionals) and AFP (Toronto and Canada South).

She currently sits on the APRA International Board of Directors, is a member of the APRA Ethics Committee and is Co-Chairing the 2014 APRA Canada conference. She had served on the APRA Canada Board of Directors and was a past Executive member for LRFRE (London Region Fund Raising Executives).

ED SLUGA is one of Canada's most experienced planned giving professionals and is currently a Managing Consultant for PGgrowth. For over 15 years, he has helped hundreds of organizations develop and benefit from long-term, sustainable and proactive fundraising and planned giving programs. Focusing on developing organizational structures and operations so that they are positioned to experience success for the long-term, Ed's chief motivation is helping organizations achieve the goals of their mission within their communities.

Ed was the associate publisher of the industry-leading manual *Planned Giving: Making it Happen* written by the late Dr. Edward Pearce and Sherry Clodman, the editor of *Canadian Gift Planning Journal*, and the co-author of *Worthy and Prepared*.

Serving international, national, regional and local not-for-profits, Ed has also provided expertise and support in various areas of organizational development, major gifts and fundraising. These include: strategic planning, organizational vision development, program creation and implementation, capacity audits and program building, action and marketing plans, professional advisor programs, marketing and communication strategies and implementation and development program audits.

GEORGE STANOIS is an acknowledged nonprofit sector leader with an extensive and accomplished consulting background. He began his fundraising career in 1984 with an international consulting firm and after gaining further experience with two national consulting companies with an emphasis on capital campaigns, he joined The Goldie Company in 1996.

A graduate of the University of Toronto, George earned his Certified Fund Raising Executive (CFRE) designation in 1990. He has been an active participant with the Association for Healthcare Philanthropy (AHP) and the Association of Fundraising Professionals (AFP) and is frequently asked to speak to organizations on the 12-Step Fundraising program. Over the years, George has served as a volunteer and board member for many charitable organizations.

George is also the author of *Dodging Tough Times: How Stewardship Programs Can Make All the Difference*, containing the results and conclusions of a 2010 survey of the major donor cultivation and recognition practices of charities in Canada. In 2009 George, together with Collis Reed Research, published *The Current State of Non-Profit Charitable Organizations in Western Canada*.

JOHN VANDUZER, President and Creative Director of wishart, is one of the most accomplished and award-winning creatives in Canada, having won well over 200 awards. He credits his success not just to his staff and clients, but to his wife and four kids who are forever asking, "are we there yet?" Ever searching for new and better ideas, John is always thinking; always creating the greater good.

A "student of advertising," John started as an account guy working at three of Canada's largest ad agencies, helping lead some of their biggest accounts (including Pepsi, Ford Motor Company and Procter & Gamble). John then traded his suit for some sandals. To the horror of small children, he's *worn both (with socks) ever since. And although it may be a fashion faux pas, this dual focus on strategic excellence coupled with creative brilliance has enabled wishart to create so*me of the sector's most iconic images and campaigns, and more importantly has helped Canadian charities raise more than one BILLION dollars in the past decade.

In his "spare time," John is a licenced lay worship leader filling in for ministers when they're away on holidays or at conferences. He is the author of the soon-to-be-published book, *Loonie*, a rollicking good tale that helps people reconcile their faith with their finances and experience grace rather than be saddled with guilt.

JIM WATSON has managed and supervised studies and major capital campaigns and programs throughout Western Canada and the Northwest Territories. He has extensive experience in all facets of fundraising, both professionally and as a volunteer. Before moving into a career as a professional fundraiser, Jim spent more than 25 years in the broadcast communications industry.

As a volunteer, Jim chaired the epic Rick Hansen Man in Motion World Tour and continued to serve on the Board of the Rick Hansen Foundation for over 25 years. He is an active member of Rotary International and a Life member of the Association of Kinsmen Clubs. In addition, Jim served as the Canadian Kinsmen National President, and he has served on the Executive of the Association of Fundraising Professionals (AFP), the Association for Healthcare Philanthropy (AHP) and the Canadian Association of Gift Planners (CAGP), as volunteer CEO of the Kinsmen Rehabilitation Foundation of BC, and has worked closely with a number of other groups and organizations.

Jim not only talks the talk, he "walks the walk" with a strong dedication to volunteerism, demonstrated on a daily basis. Jim's knowledge of, and experience in, the philanthropic community of the Lower Mainland Region and all of Western Canada is second-to-none.

VICTORIA WHITE is the owner of The Virtual Writer™, a web-based communications company that has been providing writing, editing and consulting services to clients across Canada and around the world since 2002. Specializing in the Case for Support document for The Goldie Company, she has written numerous Cases as well as collateral materials such as major gift letters for an astonishingly diverse range of not-for-profit clients and their missions. These include hospitals, colleges, community foundations, national associations, munici-palities and grassroots organizations.

Victoria is a member of the Professional Writers Asso-ciation of Canada (PWAC), the Editors' Association of Canada (EAC) and the Modern Languages Association of America (MLA). She earned two Arts degrees from the University of Western Ontario and taught at the University of Guelph for a number of years. She recently co-founded the Glanworth Community Association to ensure the preservation of the built and natural heritage of the area in which she currently lives and received a Queen's Diamond Jubilee Medal in recognition of her contribution to local community development.

INDEX

Visit **THEVIGILANTFUNDRAISER.COM**